Glenda's Story

LED BY GRACE

Glenda Revell

GATEWAY
TO JOY

Box 82500
Lincoln, NE 68501

32,000 printed to date—1997
(1170-289—10M—57)
ISBN 0-8474-1154-0

Printed in the United States of America.

I waited patiently for the LORD; he turned to me and heard my cry.

He lifted me out of the slimy pit, out of the mud and mire; he set my feet on a rock and gave me a firm place to stand.

He put a new song in my mouth, a hymn of praise to our God. Many will see and fear and put their trust in the LORD.

Psalm 40:1–3

To
Elisabeth Elliot Gren,
who was given by
the Father
to make my life
complete

Acknowledgements

I owe a debt of thanks to many special people. Some made lasting impressions in my days as a young Christian, setting my feet on the path of commitment and surrender to God. Some have been faithfully cheering me on through the years, and some are even now offering the encouragement, help and support so needed in getting this story on its way. God has used each one to impact my life and, thus, this narrative.

I would like to express my sincere gratitude and deep appreciation to some of these dear children of God:

David, who, without a thought for himself, has compassed me about with sacrificial love and understanding.

Charlotte, Sarah, Jason and Daniel, who have taught me to cherish life.

Lowell, who so many years ago had the vision to do in Christian broadcasting what "couldn't be done."

Harold and Charlotte, who cared enough to disciple me.

Lillian, who gave love, furniture and lasting friendship.

Billy and Barbara, who have sustained me with their love and inspired me with their lives.

Betty, who first encouraged me to relate these secrets of my heart.

My spiritual mother, who has shown me so much of God.

Lars, who graciously took care of details without being asked.

Mary Sue, my faithful friend, who so freely gives of herself, her time and her typing skills.

All of those at Back to the Bible who have indulgently overlooked my inexperience and kindly assisted, advised and encouraged me.

Always and above all, thanks and praise be to God, our loving Father, and to Jesus Christ, His Son, who gave Himself for us all that every life might have joyful purpose; every life story, a happy ending.

I Am His and He Is Mine

Loved with everlasting love,
Led by grace that love to know—
Spirit, breathing from above,
Thou hast taught me it is so!
O this full and perfect peace,
O this transport all divine—
In a love which cannot cease,
I am His and He is mine.

—Wade Robinson

Contents

Foreword   13

Preface   15

1. Held Up From the Womb   19
2. Tossed About   25
3. In the Night Watches   29
4. A Wicked Heart   33
5. Who Are You?   39
6. Fantasies, Hymns and Solitude   45
7. Surprise!   51
8. Changes and Choices   65
9. Starved for Love   69
10. The First Day of Life   79
11. Nothing Shall Offend   93
12. River of Pleasures   101
13. Beauty for Ashes   119

Foreword

Abandonment, abortion, abuse, addiction, adultery, alcoholism, alienation, anorexia—words hardly understood a few generations ago but now on everyone's tongue, words we can hardly escape if we pick up a newspaper or turn on television. It is generally taken for granted that these sins and sorrows can be dealt with only by law, or by something we heard little about years ago—counseling. The results of such measures are not always brilliant.

Glenda's Story, comprising all of those "A" words, reveals the wondrous efficacy of a far older answer, an answer far less frequently sought today except as a desperate venture—the Cross of Jesus. Remember the experience of Christian in *Pilgrim's Progress?*

> *He came at a place somewhat ascending; and upon that place stood a Cross, and a little below, in the bottom, a Sepulchre. So I saw in my dream, that just as Christian came up with the Cross, his burden loosed from off his shoulders, and fell from off his back, and began to tumble; and so continued to do, till it came to the mouth of the Sepulchre, where it fell in, and I saw it no more.*
>
> *Then was Christian glad and lightsome, and said, with a merry heart, "He hath given me rest by His sorrow, and life by His death."*

Glenda, just a little girl, had no idea that her sufferings were common. She carried the heavy baggage of guilt and fear, had never heard of counseling and would not have known where to turn if she had. Her story, horrifying proof of the reality of sin and of the perils of living in a broken world, carries us up and out into the radiance of a loving Father who knew her heart, saw her tears and through His amazing grace led her to that old, rugged Cross, of which is said what cannot be said of anything else in the whole world— "it is the power of God for the salvation of everyone who believes" (Rom. 1:16).

In the twentieth century, as in the first, God chooses the weak things of this world to shame the strong; He chooses the lowly, even the despised things. The wisdom of this age, He tells us, is "coming to nothing." There is another wisdom, revealed in the following pages— "foolishness" to those who have not God's Spirit—yet "no mind has conceived what God has prepared for those who love Him" (1 Cor. 2:9).

How very little Glenda knew! What chance did she have of learning? How much human help was available to her? What power drew her, all alone, to that church on Sunday mornings, or to sit under that weeping willow and talk to God? Her simple witness speaks clearly and joyfully—there is no corner of earth where the Light of the World may not shine, no heart too wounded to be opened and healed, no evil that our Lord Jesus cannot conquer.

—Elisabeth Elliot Gren
Magnolia, Massachusetts

Preface

If this were just a story about my suffering, it would be ordinary, for suffering is as commonplace as life itself. Rather, this is my account of an extraordinary Savior, who brings light out of darkness, joy out of sorrow, peace out of pain. "You turned my wailing into dancing; you removed my sackcloth and clothed me with joy, that my heart may sing to you and not be silent. O LORD my God, I will give you thanks forever" (Ps. 30:11–12).

Since this is God's story, not mine, I have relied upon His help in telling it. I have trusted Him to keep me as perfectly honest as possible. Memories are sometimes vague. I have tried to include only those remembrances that are clear to me, that I might not color the story with subjective illusions. The omission of minute detail in relating some of my most painful experiences was necessary, I felt, for "it is shameful even to mention what the disobedient do in secret" (Eph. 5:12).

It is my conviction that God has never retracted or qualified His commandment to "honor your father and your mother" (Ex. 20:12). I have walked a tightrope in this area, for in no way do I desire to dishonor the memory of my parents. How they must have suffered a private pain! My only sorrow is that I could not make it up to them.

My prayer is that God will use my story to encourage and strengthen someone who has a similar past and by this to glorify Him. There is a huge risk in this for me, for my soul is laid bare in these pages. Suppose my effort comes to nothing and no one is helped? Still, I will have obeyed. Is God not able to keep what I have committed unto Him?

As this story of my life and of my Father's love unfolds, please do not waste a shred of pity or sorrow on my behalf, for my Father has dealt bountifully with me (Ps. 142:7) and will perfect that which concerns me (Ps. 138:8).

Day by Day

Every day the Lord Himself is near me
With a special mercy for each hour;
All my cares He fain would bear, and cheer me,
He whose name is Counselor and Power.
The protection of His child and treasure
Is a charge that on Himself He laid;
"As thy days, thy strength shall be in measure,"
This the pledge to me He made.

—Lina Sandell

Chapter 1

Held Up From
the Womb

In 1951 an unwanted baby, conceived outside of marriage, was born to a family in Portsmouth, Virginia. The ensuing chaos destroyed the lives of the mother, her husband and their ten-year-old daughter.

That same year Jim Elliot wrote,

> *Granted, fate and tragedy, aimlessness and just-missing-by-a-hair are part of human experience, but they are not all, and I'm not sure they are a major part, even in the lives of men who know no Designer or design. For me, I have seen a keener force yet, the force of Ultimate Good working through apparent ill. Not that there is rosiness ever; there is genuine ill, struggle, dark-handed, unreasoning fate, mistakes, if-onlys, and all the Hardyisms you can muster. But in them I am beginning to discover a Plan greater than any could imagine.*[1]

This is not a story about the dark dealings of fate but about the marvelous works of a loving God. It is not a tale of rejection and despair (though they are participants in the

---

[1.] Elisabeth Elliot, *Shadow of the Almighty*, (New York: Harper & Row, 1989).

saga) but of deliverance and hope, everlasting love and grace, and ultimate good. It is the story of my life, for I was that illegitimate baby girl, and I have seen God overrule.

"For you have been my hope, O Sovereign LORD, my confidence since my youth. From birth I have relied on you; you brought me forth from my mother's womb" (Ps. 71:5–6).

If these events were taking place today as opposed to the 1950s, there probably would be no story to tell. My mother would have had a "choice." As it was, she nearly went to a back-alley abortionist, but after hearing some repugnant stories, she changed her mind at the last minute. Later in the pregnancy she was overwhelmed with regret and attempted to jump out of a moving car. She was held back by her sister (I called her "Aunty," and she related many of these incidents to me years later when I asked her), and we were saved. God's gracious intervention in my life had begun.

My mother was 40 years old when she discovered she was pregnant with me. She had been married for 12 years, though she and her husband were not living as man and wife. They had one child, Susan*, who was 10 years old. A casual observer would have thought them happy. But something was seriously wrong. My mother had gone from being a "social" drinker to a moderate-to-heavy drinker. And in spite of the Christian values she was taught as a child, she became promiscuous.

Susan has told me what she remembers of those years. She recalls that they were relatively happy and carefree. She was especially close to her father. When our mother

---

*name has been changed

began drinking heavily, her mean-spirited disposition grew worse. Susan remembers being taken to town on the bus and being left in the lounge of the Naval Officer's Club (ours was a Navy town) while mother disappeared with a man for long periods of time. She has vivid memories of these experiences, and I wonder how strongly they have affected her course. My sister has been married and divorced four times, and today her life is full of bitterness, loneliness and misery.

As her pregnancy progressed, my mother sank into depression, drank heavily and smoked continuously. She must have been overwhelmed by guilt, and surely there were many "if-onlys." Then another blow struck.

My mother had been fun-loving as a girl and very attractive. She had gleaming brunette hair and dark brown eyes, and she enjoyed sporting a deep bronze tan. Even at 40 she still relished the compliments she received on her beautiful skin. It was a terrible shock to her, therefore, when she woke one morning in her sixth month of pregnancy with milky white patches all over her face, neck, arms, hands and legs. She had developed vitiligo, a skin disorder in which melanin formation is inhibited. (The white patches no longer contain pigment and are sharply demarcated with hyper-pigmented borders.) It is disfiguring, and there is no cure. I believe this crushed my mother's spirit. And it stoked the fire of resentment toward her unborn, for she always believed that the pregnancy somehow caused her vitiligo.

Meanwhile, her husband had adjustments to make for himself. That the child was not his was a given. Why he continued to stay is a mystery. He was actually an easygoing person who had fallen out of love with his increasingly difficult wife long before, but he cherished Susan. His devotion to her far outweighed his disgust and anger over my mother's infidelity. He was also so profoundly lacking in initiative that I don't believe he could have left. He was a trapped man.

On February 14, 1951, I was delivered by Caesarean section, and I did not breathe. The doctor and nurses resuscitated me and kept me in an incubator for two weeks, where I improved and began to thrive. In spite of the dangerous environment of my gestation, I was healthy.

My biological father had long since fled. I never saw his face or heard his name. Perhaps he never even knew about me. But my Father knew, and He upheld me.

All Things Work Out for Good

All things work out for good, we know—
Such is God's great design;
He orders all our steps below
For purposes divine.

. . . . . .

Some day the path He chose for me
Will all be understood;
In heaven's clearer light I'll see
All things work'd out for good.

—John W. Peterson

Chapter 2

Tossed About

"Though my father and my mother forsake me,
the LORD will receive me" (Ps. 27:10).

With my biological father removed from the story, it is simpler for me to refer to my mother's husband as my father and to Susan as my sister. My father gave me his name and provided the necessities of life for me, for which I will always be grateful.

During the first five years of my life, I was frequently in the care of my father's brother Bob* and his wife, Edith.* This occurred, for the most part, when my mother was hospitalized for treatment of bleeding ulcers (two or three times a year). She was usually in the hospital for extended periods, being "dried out" while receiving special diets and medications for her peptic ulcers. Those weeks were a wonderful reprieve for me.

My father's family was from central Pennsylvania. There were five brothers raised in a small upstairs apartment in near poverty. Three of the brothers remained in Pennsylvania all of their lives, but Bob, who had recently married, moved to southeastern Virginia around 1936 seeking employment. He had heard that there were many jobs available at the Norfolk Naval Ship Yard, and he secured one as soon as he arrived. He wrote home urging his youngest brother, my father, to come and settle there.

---

*names have been changed

Employment was scarce at that time, so my father, an apprenticed machinist, came at once and was also employed at the NNSY. Both brothers remained there until retirement.

I remember Uncle Bob as a tall, burly, loud man with a big smile. He was fascinated with trains and had a huge electric train set up in his attic. How I longed to go up and see those trains, but he never asked me. He probably thought a little girl would have no interest in trains, and I was too shy to ask him.

Aunt Edith was quiet and very pretty. Her calmness soothed me. She was not at all affectionate, but I was not accustomed to affection. She took good care of me.

I distinctly remember one afternoon when Aunt Edith was cooking beets. I was playing "hospital" with a neighborhood child, and my aunt supplied us with copious amounts of beet juice "medicine." We were thrilled with the idea and medicated each other repeatedly all afternoon. We must have consumed a gallon of the stuff. To this day I cannot look at a beet square on, but the memory of that childhood play is one of my dearest and brightest.

My aunt also had some pictures taken of me, which are among the very few of my childhood.

I do not like to imagine what might have happened to me in those early years if God had not intervened on my behalf. My aunt and uncle, though not even blood relatives, provided a solace for me in their home. When I was at my home, I was sometimes beaten savagely. At age three, my two front teeth were knocked out. I don't remember much about the beatings, but I remember the absence of those teeth for four years.

I was removed from the sanctuary of my uncle's home when I was about five. I recall my father and Uncle Bob arguing. They exchanged harsh words. Perhaps my aunt and uncle were weary of the responsibility of caring for someone else's child. I really don't know why they took me in in the first place. But now it was time to leave the refuge of their home and enter the refuge, yet unknown to me, of the shadow of God's wings. He, rather than man, became my Deliverer. In His arms He took me up.

Praise Ye the Lord, the Almighty

Praise ye the Lord, who with
marvelous wisdom hath made thee,
Decked thee with health, and with
loving hand guided and stayed thee;
How oft in grief
Hath not He brought thee relief,
Spreading His wings for to shade thee!

—Joachim Neander

Chapter 3

In the Night Watches

"O God, you are my God, earnestly I seek you;
my soul thirsts for you, my body longs for you,
in a dry and weary land where there is no water. . . .

"My soul will be satisfied as with the richest of foods;
with singing lips my mouth will praise you.

"On my bed I remember you; I think of you through
the watches of the night. Because you are my help,
I sing in the shadow of your wings" (Ps. 63:1, 5-7).

I do not remember a time when I did not believe in God. Where I first heard of Him I cannot fathom, but thinking of Him and praying to Him are among my earliest memories.

My concept of God was imperfect, for I knew nothing of Jesus Christ or the Holy Spirit, but I somehow knew He is powerful, fearsome and good. It did not enter my mind that He is loving, and I would not have dared think He would deign to love *me*. Yet somehow He drew me, and I longed for Him.

My family lived in a tiny, four-room house built during World War II. The homes in our community were modest, intended only to provide temporary shelter for shipyard workers. But most of them are still standing today.

I suppose we were poor. We never owned a car. Our little house was heated by an oil-burning stove, which stood in the living room. My father's shoes were always lined with cardboard because of the huge holes in the soles. He worked very hard—sometimes seven days a week—and long hours. I suspect my mother's drinking and subsequent hospitalizations soaked up an inordinate share of his income. However, I do not recall lacking food or adequate clothing.

There were two small bedrooms in the house. We called one the front room and the other the back room. The front room was considered to be my parents' bedroom, although my mother had slept on the living room couch for years. My sister and I shared a double bed in the back room.

When I came home from my uncle's house for the last time, a devastating change was made. My sister, then 15, was moved to the front room to sleep with our mother. I was to sleep in the back room with my father. I have no idea whether or not there were any objections. It wouldn't have mattered. My mother made the decisions and gave the commands. We followed them.

Anyone can imagine what might result from such circumstances: a man whose needs had not been met for years, sleeping with a little girl, not his own, while trying to cope with long days of hard work and an alcoholic wife.

In that little room my innocence was mutilated over and over again. The physical pain, the fear and the shame were unspeakable. The knowledge that there was nowhere to go, no one to tell, horrified me. I wanted to run, but he held me down; I wanted to scream, but he told me I must be quiet. So over the years, in that desolate bed, I learned to cry out to God. With tears running back into my ears and my father asleep at my side, I stared at the ceiling and prayed.

"Listen to my prayer, O God, do not ignore my plea; hear me and answer me. My thoughts trouble me and I am distraught at the voice of the enemy, at the stares of the wicked; for they bring down suffering upon me and revile me in their anger. My heart is in anguish within me; the terrors of death assail me. Fear and trembling have beset me; horror has overwhelmed me" (Ps. 55:1–5).

In those lonely hours I began to meditate on God. Who was He? Where was He? How could I get to Him? I concluded that He would surely answer my prayers if only I would be good. When no relief came and the beatings and sexual abuse continued, I was convinced it was because I was so bad.

But I continued praying, and in those troubled times, in the night watches, God became more and more real to me. He covered me with His outspread wings. My affliction became the cord with which He drew me to Himself.

"It was good for me to be afflicted so that I might learn your decrees" (Ps. 119:71).

God Is in This

God is in this and every place;
But O, how dark and void
To me!— 'tis one great wilderness
This earth without my God.

Empty of Him who all things fills,
Till He His light impart,—
Till He His glorious self reveals,—
The veil is on my heart.

O Thou who seest and know'st my grief,
Thyself unseen, unknown,
Pity my helpless unbelief,
And break my heart of stone.

—Charles Wesley

Chapter 4

A Wicked Heart

Today it is fashionable, almost desirable, to be a victim. Everyone has a story, and no one can be outdone when it comes to how severely he has been abused. Even in Christian circles this is a popular theme. The attitude that dominates these tales of woe is, "Someone has violated me and intruded on my rights. Having endured this commends me, makes me special to God. He is now, or will be or should be giving me the peace, happiness, contentment and success that were rightfully mine all along."

Such thinking is seriously flawed because it is based on the false supposition that humans are innately good and therefore deserving of only the best life has to offer. If we are willing, however, to be confronted by the truth of Scripture, we must reach a far different conclusion:

> "The heart is deceitful above all things and beyond cure" (Jer. 17:9).

> "There is no one righteous, not even one" (Rom. 3:10).

> "All have sinned and fall short of the glory of God" (Rom. 3:23).

In honesty, we must confess that we merit judgment

rather than pity. We have sinned against a holy God more than our victimizers have sinned against us.

As our eyes are opened to this astonishing reality, we must then wonder why God has withheld judgment against us for so long. In fact, His fierce judgment has not been restrained but has fallen on Jesus, who knew no sin. "Surely he took up our infirmities and carried our sorrows. . . . he was pierced for our transgressions, he was crushed for our iniquities; the punishment that brought us peace was upon him, and by his wounds we are healed" (Isa. 53:4–5).

Therefore, it should be our own vile sin, committed against a holy God and for which Christ suffered, that fills us with sorrow and remorse—not the sin that others commit against us.

That's why my most painful memories are not of the abuse I suffered but of the wickedness of my own heart. Apart from the restraining power of Christ, I would be far worse than my tormentors ever were. He alone has kept me from iniquity. My rights were never violated the way His were. I was never beaten the way He was. I was never subjected to the rejection and derision that He endured.

Would to God that we could have a glimpse of what we *really* deserve. Of course, we can if we are willing to gaze upon the cross.

"For I know my transgressions, and my sin is always before me. Against you, you only, have I sinned and done what is evil in your sight, so that you are proved right when you speak and justified when you judge" (Ps. 51:3-4).

Outwardly I was compliant and obedient as a child. I desperately wanted to please someone and to be loved. But that was not a reflection of inner goodness, nor did I have a submissive heart. Actually, by the time I was six years old, I was so filled with hatred that I committed murder in my heart.

At times my mother would catch the afternoon bus to town, where she would barhop all evening. She would then catch the last bus back home around 1:00 a.m. These excursions irritated my father, and he would always get out of bed when she finally staggered in the door. (Once, he locked her out.) Then there would be a horrible fight.

The screaming, cursing and arguing that ensued were unbearable to hear. I remember the burning knot in my throat and the intense pain in my stomach as I listened. I would lie in bed with a pillow pulled tightly over my face, crying my heart out but not daring to make a sound. This awful scene was repeated over and over again throughout my childhood.

I distinctly remember one of those nights. The fight was over, and my father had come back to bed and fallen asleep. As always, my mother went immediately to sleep, and I could hear her snoring from the front room. I was overwhelmed with hatred for her. It makes me shudder to remember this, but the thought occurred to me that I could just kill her. I pictured myself going into the kitchen, getting a knife, slipping into my mother's room and stabbing her. I *wanted* to do it.

As I lay there contemplating murder, I thought, *I am only six years old. If I kill her, I will have to go to jail for the rest of my life. That would be a long time in jail.* I must have decided it wasn't worth it. I closed my eyes and went to sleep. But God never allowed me to forget those wicked imaginings, and I became increasingly aware of my sinfulness.

I also practiced a lot of deception. Deceiving my family and classmates was routine for me. By the time I was eight years old, for example, I knew just how much vodka, gin and whiskey I could pour down the sink while my mother slept without her noticing it the next morning. I hoped this would keep her from getting as drunk the next day.

Whenever a classmate asked to come by my house on the way home, I made up wild stories to keep her away. "My mother told me she is waxing all the floors today, so I can't have anyone in" was one of them. I told my friends anything but the truth. Once when a teacher asked why my parents did not attend the PTA meeting, I told her it was because my mother was in the hospital. She wasn't. Another time I told a girl who wanted to come to my house that my mother had a terrible disease and if she came in she might catch it. "You didn't catch it," she retorted.

The trouble is, I did. It was the malady common to the human race—sin. And I felt hopeless to overcome it.

O Jesus, Thou Art Standing

O Jesus, Thou art knocking—
And lo! that hand is scarred,
And thorns Thy brow encircle,
And tears Thy face have marred:
O love that passeth knowledge,
So patiently to wait!
O sin that has no equal,
So fast to bar the gate!

—William W. How

Chapter 5

Who Are You?

Poor I may be—despised, forgot,
Yet God, my God, forgets me not;
And he is safe and must succeed,
For whom the Savior deigns to plead.

—William Cowper

A sense of not belonging anywhere or to anyone pervaded my childhood. Even my appearance was a hindrance—a blue-eyed towhead in the midst of brown-eyed brunettes. I remember being out with my father and hearing comments such as, "Where in the world did you get her? From the milkman?" Perhaps that is why the following incident caused me so much pain that I can still feel its sting.

As I mentioned before, Susan confronted enormous heartache and difficulty after my birth. She had lost a mother to alcoholism, and I think it may have been worse for her than for me because she could remember how it "used to be." The family had disintegrated. It was natural that she associated all of this pain and misery with me. She became bitter and vicious; still, I pity her. Who knows how different her life would have been had I not been born.

Since we did not own a car, my mother ordered the bulk of our groceries from a local grocer who delivered. We walked to one of two nearby stores to buy whatever we ran out of between orders.

Late one chilly afternoon, my sister, who was 15 at the time, was sent to the store, and I tagged along. The trip was about a mile each way, and, as a preschooler, I did not know the way alone. Susan was aware of this. As soon as we were out of sight of our house, she looked at me with disdain and said, "Who are you? I don't know you." At first I just laughed and said, "Of course you know me. I'm your sister." She did not back down. "You're not my sister," she exclaimed. "I've never seen you before in my life!"

After several minutes of this, I panicked and begged her to stop. She ignored my plea. "Get away from me! I'm telling you I don't know you."

All the way to the store, through the store and back home, I followed her from what I thought was a safe distance. It was getting dark, and I was terrified that I would lose sight of her and be lost. But worse than the fear was the confusion and the pain I felt. "I'm Glenda. I'm your sister," I kept shouting ahead to her. She would occasionally turn her head around, never breaking her stride, and shout back to me, "I told you to leave me alone! I don't know you!"

With my short legs it was impossible for me to keep up with her. Running intermittently left me gasping for air. I could see my panting breath in the cold evening air, and I felt chilled to the bone. When we finally turned the last corner and I caught sight of our little house, I was overcome with relief and started to cry. That house had never been a symbol of security to me before, but that night I could not wait to get inside, to find that what I knew to be real was real.

With renewed energy I picked up speed. Susan made

it into the house a few seconds ahead of me. Once inside, I slammed the door behind me and leaned on it, panting, looking around the living room, trying to find comfort in familiar surroundings.

Susan emerged from the kitchen into the living room where I stood, with mother close behind her. The contemptuous grins on their faces bewildered and frightened me. My sister pointed to me and said, "See, there she is. She followed me all the way home." Mother looked at me and commented, "You're right. I've never seen her before either." Then she turned on her heels and went back into the kitchen. My sister went to the front room to do her homework, giving me a sardonic smile as she passed. I was left standing there, gaping and wounded and completely alone, I thought, in the world.

"You know how I am scorned, disgraced and shamed; all my enemies are before you. Scorn has broken my heart and has left me helpless; I looked for sympathy, but there was none, for comforters, but I found none" (Ps. 69:19–20).

Sexual defilement of a child is a monstrous sin, and the rape of a child's spirit is on equal footing. The damage from either would appear irreversible. But as Dr. David Jeremiah has said, "Our God has the power to reverse the irreversible."[1] It is true, for I have tasted of His cure from both, and it fills me with a longing for Him that the happiest of childhoods could not have given.

---

[1] from David Jeremiah's radio program, *Turning Point*

Each care, each ill of mortal birth
Is sent in pitying love,
To lift the ling'ring heart from earth,
And speed its flight above.
And every pang that wrings the breast,
And every joy that dies,
Tell us to seek a purer rest,
And trust to holier ties.

—James Montgomery

Thy Gracious Presence

Thy gracious presence, O my God,
All that I wish contains;
With this, beneath affliction's load,
My heart no more complains.

Lord, shall the breathings of my heart
Aspire in vain to Thee?
Confirm my hope that where Thou art
I shall forever be.

Then shall my cheerful spirit sing
The darksome hours away,
And rise, on faith's expanded wing
To everlasting day.

—Ann Steele

Chapter 6

Fantasies, Hymns and Solitude

"The LORD watches over you—
the LORD is your shade at your right hand;
the sun will not harm you by day,
nor the moon by night.

"The LORD will keep you from all harm—
he will watch over your life;
the LORD will watch over your coming and
going both now and forevermore" (Ps. 121:5–8).

A huge weeping willow tree transformed our otherwise uninteresting, tiny yard into my private fantasyland. In summer, its full branches swept the ground, and underneath that leafy umbrella I felt safe, contented and close to God, untouched by the chaos and struggle in the house just a few feet away. I spent countless hours beneath those sheltering branches playing with dolls, coloring and drawing and, oddly enough, singing praises to the God I did not yet know.

Could Almighty God care enough about me that He would plant a willow tree years before my conception to shelter me from the storms of life beneath its lithe branches? I know it to be true—this and an infinite number of mercies He extended to me.

"The LORD is my strength and my shield; my heart trusts in him, and I am helped. My heart leaps for joy and I will give thanks to him in song" (Ps. 28:7).

School also was a wonderful reprieve from the trauma of my home life. I loved it. I became an avid reader. I requested more and more books from my teachers because there were no books at home, and I loved the escape they provided. Art class was my favorite, and I developed creativity and an eye for color. I loved playing with other children, although I always felt inferior to them. This did not cause me much anguish; I just accepted it as truth and carried on.

All those school memories had a lasting impact on my life, but nothing affected me more than my hours of solitude beneath the willow tree. There, my life was sweet and well ordered, a stark contrast to the rest of my world, where all I could be sure of was a lack of surety.

My imagination was also a gift from God. I often fantasized about a mother who deeply loved me. She kissed me good night and read me stories (my real mother never did either of those things). She was my loving, if imaginary, companion through many of those horrid years when I might have been crushed by the burden I bore.

The same year I started school I began attending the little Methodist church just a few blocks from our house. I had passed it many times on my way to the store and longed to go inside. I thought perhaps God lived there and would be more likely to answer my prayers if I prayed in church. Then I met a girl in school who attended church there. She told me about the stories she heard and the songs she sang. That was more than enough to convince me. I went home and bravely asked my mother if I could go. I fully expected her to scream at me and slap me.

Surprisingly, she said yes. How thankful I am for her consent, for the years I spent in that church were a wonderful comfort to me.

On Sunday mornings, rain or shine, I dressed myself and walked to church. Sometimes I was the first to arrive. When that happened, I just plopped myself down on the front steps and waited, full of joy and anticipation.

I wonder how I must have looked to those people. Was my hair brushed? Was I clean? What did they think of the little girl who came to Sunday school alone and sat, solitary, on the front row during the church service? Did anyone even notice? Did anyone care? I don't know the answer to any of those questions, but this I do know: I, who was particularly sensitive to the attitudes and opinions of others, never felt rejected or unwanted there. It was a marvelous place for me to grow and thrive.

Although I did not hear the Gospel preached in that church, I did hear Bible stories that laid the groundwork for my future faith. I learned to recite the Apostle's Creed and the Lord's Prayer. Most of all, I learned the precious, old hymns of the faith (all new to me): "Holy, Holy, Holy," "O for a Thousand Tongues," "Immortal, Invisible," "The Old Rugged Cross," "Trust and Obey," "Sweet Hour of Prayer" and, of course, "Jesus Loves Me." I sang them with exuberance in church, and I sang them with the same exuberance under the willow tree. I may not have understood all of the doctrine tucked in those stanzas, but I was comforted by the simple truths I did understand.

I learned God is loving, though I was sure He couldn't possibly love me. I never even thought He should. My previous concept of His power and greatness became more firmly rooted in my psyche. I learned that He is "Three

Persons." I longed to know more. And in my hours of solitude, He was with me, instructing me and guiding me
through the gift of music.

"I will sing to the LORD all my life; I will sing praise
to my God as long as I live. May my meditation be pleasing
to him, as I rejoice in the LORD" (Ps. 104:33–34).

God of My Strength

God of my strength, in Thee alone
A refuge from distress I see;
O why hast Thou Thine aid withdrawn?
Why hast Thou, Lord, forsaken me?

O let Thy light my footsteps guide;
Thy love and truth my spirit fill;
That in Thy house I may reside
And worship at Thy holy hill.

Why then, my soul, art thou cast down?
Why art thou anxious and distressed?
Hope thou in God, His mercy own,
For I shall yet enjoy His rest.

—Wrangham

Chapter 7

Surprise!

"You, O God, do see trouble and grief; you consider it
to take it in hand. The victim commits himself to you.
You are the helper of the fatherless" (Ps. 10:14).

The summer before I entered fifth grade, my
mother's behavior took an eerie turn. Although
she was drinking more than ever, she was frequenting bars
less. Most of her drinking was done at home now, and she
became a recluse, withdrawing from the real world into a
realm all her own.

Nearly all of her waking hours were spent sitting on a
bar stool alone in the darkness of our tiny kitchen. She
wore nothing but a slip, day and night. She drank, smoked
cigarettes and sometimes muttered to herself. Occasionally
she barked out orders to my father or me, but for the most
part, she didn't participate in our lives. My mother had
been reduced to not much more than an angry voice from
the kitchen. At night, all I saw of her was the red glow on
the end of her cigarette.

My father spent more and more time away from home,
working long hours every day and every weekend. I suppose that is the way he coped with this tormented woman
who so completely ruled our lives from her 7' x 9' sanc-
tum. My sister had married three years earlier and was, for
the most part, out of our lives. Loneliness engulfed me.

Guilt was my constant companion, for I believed I

was responsible for all of this misery and distress and there was nothing I could do to make it right, nowhere I could go for comfort or advice.

I still hated my mother. Not that I wanted to. The smallest display of tenderness or affection on her part would have disarmed me, and I would have loved her completely, so tenuous is the line that separates love and hate. But tenderness was not forthcoming, nor was there any love for her in my heart. Even so, I did sometimes pity her, and I longed to please her, to do something that would bring her out of her drunken, impenetrable world. Finding a remedy for my fractured family consumed me. It was a crushing load on the shoulders of a ten-year-old.

One night in late August of that year stands out from all the others. Preparing to go to bed, I hesitated outside of the kitchen doorway, dreading the nightly ritual I put myself through. As usual, the tiny glow of my mother's cigarette was all I could see as I peered into the dark kitchen. With neither of us speaking a word, I walked over to the bar stool where she was perched. She stuck out her cheek, and I kissed it. Then she waved me away with her hand, and I quickly exited, wishing I could exit as easily from her life. I knew she wished the same.

This would have been no different from any other night except for one thing—my father was later than usual coming to bed, so I had time to think. *What can I do to make Mother love me? What would make her happy?*

Suddenly I was struck with a wonderful idea. *Of course! Why didn't I think of it before? I'll give her a birthday party! Her birthday isn't until November. I'll have plenty of time. But no, she'll never let me do it. She'll think I don't know how. Well, I'll just give her a surprise*

*party! I can do it. I know I can! I've been to birthday parties
before. There's nothing to it: cake, ice cream, balloons,
games. It will be great fun, and she'll love it. She'll love me!*

Hasty thoughts tumbled through my mind as my
excitement mounted.

*Oh, but wait a minute. Parties cost money, and I
don't have any money. Where can I get some?* This problem quickly dampened my spirits, but only for a moment.

*That's it! My lunch money. Let's see. When school
starts, I'll have 30 cents a day for lunch. By November 11
I'll have, hmm . . .* I got out of bed to retrieve a calendar
and some paper. *Wow! I'll have about $14. I can give a
great party with all that money.*

This was the best idea I ever had. I couldn't remember
having been so happy.

"Dear God," I prayed, "help me to give a good party
for Mother. And make her stop drinking. Oh, and make
her love me if You can. Amen."

The school year started, and I faithfully saved my
lunch money each day. I don't remember being particularly
hungry from all those skipped lunches. Every now and
then, someone would give me an apple or a cookie or a
sandwich he didn't like. Hunger wasn't much of a burden
to bear, anyway, compared to the hunger of soul and spirit
I had borne all of my life. The love I was anticipating
would be well worth any sacrifice.

As the days grew shorter and cooler, my plan became
specific and more detailed. How to get Mother out of the
house on her birthday so I could make preparations per-
plexed me. After considering different scenarios, I settled
on one as the least risky. *I'll have to get Aunty to help me.*

It's my only chance.

I called Aunty and, with trepidation, filled her in on the plan.

"You mustn't tell anyone, Aunty, or you'll spoil everything," I said.

She seemed to think the party was a fine idea and pledged her help. Because November 11 fell on a Saturday that year, it made everything easier. School would be out, and Aunty would be off work. She would invite Mother and Daddy out for lunch to celebrate Mother's birthday, and I would have everything ready by their return.

At first Mother turned down the proposal, saying that a 50th birthday was nothing to celebrate and that she didn't feel like going out anyway. But Aunty persisted, and Mother finally agreed. *Whew! One problem solved.*

A bakery in our little community had always fascinated me with its delightful window displays and mouthwatering aroma of baking bread. I proudly entered that bakery on my way home from school in early November and plopped my bulging money sack on the counter. A plump, kind-faced, grandmotherly woman came out of a back room, wiping her flour-coated fingers on her white apron.

"Can I help you, dear?" she asked.

"I want to order a cake."

"What kind of cake?" She pulled a pencil out of her piled-up gray hair and poised to write.

"A pretty cake," I responded, wondering why she had to ask the obvious.

She patiently pointed out the various types of cakes

she baked and asked how many people I planned to serve with it.

I counted them all up on my fingers—my aunts and uncle, Mother, Daddy and me, of course, and 9 neighbors. That's 15 in all. She recommended a quarter of a sheet cake, but I had my eye on a beautiful, round, double-layer cake. She said it should do nicely if I didn't slice the pieces too big.

"I won't," I promised.

"Do you want anything written on the cake?"

"Oh, yes. Make it with pretty flowers just like that one," I pointed to a cake in the showcase, "and write 'HAPPY BIRTHDAY, MOTHER' on it."

She looked at me with such kindness in her twinkling blue eyes as I had never seen. "You have a very lucky mother," she said.

I was ecstatic. I smiled brightly at her, unable to contain my happiness.

"How much does it cost?" I began pouring my hoarded coins on the counter.

"It will be $5.50, but you can pay for it when you pick it up."

"Oh." I was embarrassed at not knowing that. I began picking up the coins and dropping them back into the sack.

"When do you want it?"

"November 11 at 12:30," I answered, happy to let this lady in on my well-kept secret. "It's a surprise."

"It'll be ready, honey," she promised.

I left the bakery feeling lighthearted and grown-up.

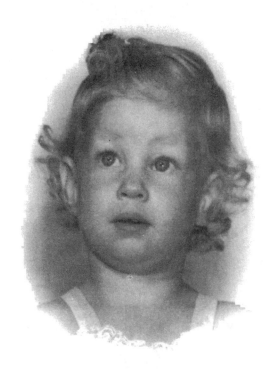

As a toddler.

The house of my
childhood as it
looks today.

Iva Ropp with me when I was 4 1/2. Iva was a neighbor whom I loved very much. She took care of me from time to time when my mother was in the hospital. She also made clothes for me. I've often wondered how much she knew about our family life. She died in 1978.

As a freshman nursing student in 1971.

David and me on
our wedding day,
April 3, 1976.

My family with Elisabeth
Elliot in 1990. (Front, left
to right) Daniel, Jason,
Charlotte and Sarah.
(Back) Me, Elisabeth,
David.

My family in October 1993.

This was truly going to be a wonderful party.

The next day after school, I walked to the dime store and bought some glass figurines to be used as prizes for the games and a bag of party balloons. I also bought tissue paper and ribbon to wrap the prizes and a birthday card—one of those big ones with satin and lace that come in a box. Everything had to be perfect.

The afternoon before the party, I went into my bedroom and closed the door. I quietly opened the dresser drawer where I had hidden the bag of balloons. I eyed them skeptically. I had never been able to blow up a balloon before. I sat down on the floor beside my bed, tore open the plastic bag and breathed a prayer: "Oh, God. Please help me blow up these balloons."

I blew up the first balloon and struggled to tie it. Then I blew up another and another until they were all done, and I sat surrounded by a dozen or more brightly colored balloons. I was delighted with my work.

When my ears stopped ringing and my peripheral vision returned, I was confronted with a new problem. Mother would surely suspect something if she found balloons all over my room. Where could I hide them? Then I saw the obvious solution—my closet.

It seemed obvious at first, but stuffing an already cramped closet with balloons was more difficult than I imagined. Two in, one out, three in, two out, BANG! *Oh, no! Did Mother hear it pop?* I held my breath and waited motionlessly for several minutes. Nothing. *Good. Now back to work, this time more carefully.*

There were no more mishaps, and eventually my delicate work was done, all balloons safely corralled for the night.

The day of my mother's birthday was sunny and unseasonably warm. *This is the day!* I threw back the covers and jumped out of bed. There was so much to do, but I couldn't start until Aunty picked up Mother and Daddy at 11:30. I kept myself occupied with dressing, brushing my teeth and making my bed, wishing that time wouldn't drag on so. My thoughts were racing when I overheard my mother on the phone.

"Let's just skip it for today," she said. "I have a headache, and I'm not up to going."

My head reeled, and my heart sank to the floor. *No, no, no! This can't be happening. She has to go!*

I don't know what kind of persuasion Aunty used, but it was powerful, for Mother finally consented to go. The luncheon was on again. *Yippee!* My knees were so weak from the sudden apprehension that I had to sit down to keep from falling.

Before long the house was empty, and I hurriedly went to work. First, I took out all the balloons and tied them with ribbon, hanging them from light fixtures and curtain rods. When I was satisfied that they looked just right, I proceeded with the next task—gingerly setting out the china dessert plates, silverware and glasses. I placed the wrapped prizes on a shelf in the dining room and set out my card, propping it up against a candy dish. I stood back and viewed the festive scene with satisfaction.

Jumping on my bike, I flew to the grocery store for the ice cream. I bought Neapolitan—something for everyone. Then I rode back home, put the ice cream in the freezer and walked to the bakery.

The cake was gorgeous! I had never seen a more wonderful cake. I paid the nice lady, and she gently placed the box in my arms. She offered me a donut for the road.

"No, thank you." I was far too excited to eat.

"That's fine. Have fun. And let me know how your mother likes her cake," she shouted after me.

Back home, I had just removed the cake from the box when the neighbors started coming.

"Come in. Everyone, come in, please. Have a seat. Aunty will be bringing my mother at 2:00, so it won't be long now."

Then Uncle Bob and Aunt Edith arrived. They parked their car around the corner and out of sight, so my mother wouldn't be suspicious. All was going well.

Moments later Aunty's '51 Chevy pulled up in front of the house.

"Everyone—shhh! Be quiet," one neighbor said.

"Yell 'surprise' when they open the door," I whispered.

A few breathless moments passed, and then . . . SURPRISE!

It was apparent from the expression on my mother's face that Aunty hadn't spilled the beans, a possibility I had feared. She was utterly shocked—so much so that she had to grab on to Aunty for support and looked as if she might faint. She was led inside and sat down. From across the room I eagerly scanned her face. Reading her every expression and mood was my specialty, but I wasn't sure this time. *Is she pleased?* She seemed to be regathering her composure somewhat. *Yes, I think she is pleased. She's just very surprised.*

I was very busy with the unfamiliar duties of being hostess. Aunty and Aunt Edith helped me serve the cake and ice cream. I noticed with disappointment that Mother declined her piece, saying she was too full from lunch. But the guests played the childish games I had planned, and there were even "oohs" and "aahs" over the little prizes. Everyone was so kind to me.

It was soon time for Mother to open her gifts. She cried when she opened Aunty's. It was an exquisite lace tablecloth. I wished I had a nice gift for her. All I had was a card. But it was an extra-special card. Maybe she wouldn't notice my lack of a gift in all the excitement. Daddy didn't give her anything. I hoped this wouldn't cause a fight later.

One by one, guests began to leave, some patting me on the head, some hugging me, all saying they had a grand time and thanking me for inviting them. I overheard some of them saying complimentary things to Mother about me. One person asked my father if he had helped me with the party. "No," he said, "I didn't know a thing about it." I'm sure I was glowing with pride. I had never done anything right before, but this had to be a success.

Aunty was the last guest to leave, and I was relieved to see the house empty at last. I turned to look at Mother, expecting a reward for all my planning, hard work and sacrifice.

At first she said nothing. I was smiling at her, waiting for a response, but my smile faded quickly when I recognized the all-too-familiar angry expression on her face. She glared at me.

"How dare you?" she snarled.

"What do you mean? Didn't you like it? Aren't you happy?"

"How could you invite all of those people into this filthy house?" she screamed. "Are you trying to ruin me?"

Filthy house? This is a filthy house?

"No, Mother," I pleaded. "I only wanted to make you happy. I thought—"

"I know all about you. You are a sneaky, conniving girl, always scheming, trying to ruin me!"

I was stunned at her reaction, unable to respond. *This can't be happening. I'm dreaming.*

Daddy walked past me and slipped out the front door. As usual, he left me to deal with her alone.

She spoke through clenched teeth, "You get in there and clean up every bit of the mess. Go!" She shoved me against the table. "Get out of my sight!"

Numbly, I did as she ordered, picking up napkins, washing dishes and straightening chair cushions. Crumbs on the dining room table were all that was left of my beautiful cake. As I cleaned up the remaining mess, the shock and numbness wore off, and hot tears began pouring down my face. I couldn't wait to get to the privacy of my room.

Exhausted, I fell face first on the bed, sobbing, aching, overwhelmed with grief. Then it hit me—the awful realization that I had failed again. I had given all I had. I was completely spent. But it wasn't enough. I would never be good enough to be loved. Never. There was nothing more I could do. I was swallowed up in hopelessness.

"Save me, O God, for the waters have come up to my neck. I sink in the miry depths, where there is no foothold.

I have come into the deep waters; the floods engulf me. I am worn out calling for help; my throat is parched. My eyes fail, looking for my God" (Ps. 69:1–3).

Fatigue eventually overcame me, and I ran out of tears. I tried to imagine my pretend mother kissing me good night, comforting me with kind words, but she wouldn't come. Even my imagination failed me.

I lay there all night in my best dress and shiny black shoes, sunk in the deep, troubled sleep that often accompanies great sorrow. I don't know where my father slept that night, but he didn't sleep with me. I was glad to be alone with my pain.

On the surface, my life changed little because of that terrible day. Mother kept on drinking. Daddy kept on working late and sleeping with me at night. I continued to go to school, but at least I was able to eat lunch again. Everything was pretty much the same.

In the unseen realm, however, my failure made a profound impact on my future thinking and behavior. I could no longer trust my judgment. I had thought—been sure even—that the party was a good idea. Clearly, it hadn't been. So I was left unable to make any decision with confidence. There was a constant undercurrent of doubt and a gripping fear that I would repeat my stupid performance.

My attitude toward my mother changed as well. Not that it had ever been good, but there *had* been hope. Now I knew that she could never really love me or be a mother to me. I never tried to please her again in the same, old way I had always tried. It was hopeless. Mostly, I just stayed out of her way.

I have heard people ask, "How can God be loving and

kind when He allows such suffering in the lives of innocent children?" The answer lies in perspective. As any loving parent knows, he must sometimes withhold seemingly good things for the ultimate good of his child.

Likewise, our dear Father is much more concerned with our eternal destiny than with giving us temporal pleasure. And unlike earthly fathers, God knows precisely what we need of both pain and pleasure to draw us to the ultimate good He has planned for us.

I know now that God did not forsake me during my dark night of sorrow. All the time He was drawing me to Himself by peeling away, one by one, those objects of my longing, that, if given, would have kept me from longing for Him. God was on my side. His strong arm, which, in His great wisdom, so sorely bruised me, would eventually, in merciful tenderness, gather me into His bosom.

"If the LORD had not been on our side when men attacked us, when their anger flared against us, they would have swallowed us alive; the flood would have engulfed us, the torrent would have swept over us, the raging waters would have swept us away. Praise be to the LORD, who has not let us be torn by their teeth. We have escaped like a bird out of the fowler's snare; the snare has been broken, and we have escaped. Our help is in the name of the LORD, the Maker of heaven and earth" (Ps. 124:2–8).

When All Thy Mercies, O My God

When all Thy mercies, O my God,
My rising soul surveys,
Transported with the view, I'm lost
In wonder, love and praise.

Unnumbered comforts to my soul
Thy tender care bestowed,
Before my infant heart conceived
From whom those comforts flowed.

—Joseph Addison

Chapter 8

Changes and Choices

When I was seven, my sister eloped. Life was so miserable at home that she thought anything would be better. Although we had never shared a comradeship, I felt scared and deserted when she left.

Within the first week of her marriage, Susan realized that she had made a horrible decision. Her husband was cruel and abusive. When she tried to return home she was told, "You've made your bed—now lie in it." What a hard bed it has been for her.

I was making some choices of my own during those years. Though outwardly compliant, I must have been strong-willed, because I made up my mind about many things with much resolve. I remember the circumstances surrounding these decisions so vividly that I'm certain they were potent shapers of my will and future.

At about age 12 I purposed that I would never touch a cigarette or drink alcohol. My mother's drinking binges had become more and more frequent. I despised even the thought of alcohol. It was not a bit hard to see its destructive power in her life and to feel it in mine. Alcohol and tobacco stole my mother's life away, mercilessly, one year at a time.

I also wanted desperately to be a good student. Some years were better than others. It is difficult for any child to study and learn when she bears heavy burdens and dark secrets. I tried very hard, though, and strove to please my teachers; but by the fifth, sixth and seventh grades, the struggle nearly overcame me, and I did poorly.

Because of overcrowding in the junior high school, the year I entered the eighth grade became the year I entered high school. Attending the eighth grade in a high school could have its pitfalls, but it was a great thrill to me. I was excited to go to a new school. I thought, *I have only one life, and I'm the only one who can make something out of it. I'm going to study hard, and I'm going to make straight A's. Then, even if my parents don't care about me, perhaps my teachers will like me.*

Another decision I made concerned my future family. After another episode of severe abuse, I thought, *I will never, never treat my little girl like this.*

It was clearly the Heavenly Father, "guiding me with His eye," who directed these decisions. Those choices did not originate from my unregenerate heart but from the heart of God. The One who loved me and gave Himself for me led me all the way. What grace!

The best change came when I was 12. My father moved into the front room, my mother returned to the living room couch, and I slept alone. Since I had by that time reached puberty, I suppose fear of another unwanted baby prompted the switch. But I know that it was God who moved my father out of that room.

"I will be glad and rejoice in your love, for you saw my affliction and knew the anguish of my soul. You have not handed me over to the enemy but have set my feet in a spacious place" (Ps. 31:7–8).

Other changes were not as positive. I still enjoyed singing the marvelous hymns I had learned, but I sang with less gusto than before. I still prayed every day, but more as a habit than a heart cry. I prayed ritualistically on my way to school each morning. I thought that if I spent the entire walk to school in prayer, God would keep my mother from getting drunk that day. When it didn't work, I just assumed that I had not said the right words or that I wasn't good enough for God to answer my prayers.

Much of the time my heart was heavy. I was weighted down with guilt and shame. I became preoccupied with thoughts of my worthlessness. Then, when I was 14, I lost my childhood refuge—the old willow tree died.

Be Still, My Soul

Be still, my soul—the Lord is on thy side!
Bear patiently the cross of grief or pain;
Leave to thy God to order and provide—
In ev'ry change He faithful will remain.
Be still, my soul—thy best, thy heav'nly Friend
Thru thorny ways leads to a joyful end.

—Katharina von Schlegel

Chapter 9

Starved for Love

"Turn to me and be gracious to me,
for I am lonely and afflicted.
The troubles of my heart have multiplied;
free me from my anguish.
Look upon my affliction and my distress
and take away all my sins.
See how my enemies have increased
and how fiercely they hate me!
Guard my life and rescue me;
let me not be put to shame,
for I take refuge in you" (Ps. 25:16–20).

Shelly Martin* and I had been friends since the fifth grade. Neither of us was outgoing. In fact, we were both painfully shy and quiet. Perhaps this is what drew us to one another. Whatever it was, we became fast friends. We did schoolwork and projects together. I spent the night at her house often, and we had some wonderful times together. She was my only friend.

Shelly's house was about 30 minutes' walking distance from mine, and I frequently made my way there. It was a fine house, clean and neat, and there was always the smell of something cooking wafting throughout. And the conveniences! There were two bathrooms, a dishwasher, a washing machine, a dryer and, twice a week, a maid. There

---

*name has been changed

was also an in-ground swimming pool and bathhouse in the backyard. To me, it was paradise.

What really drew me to Shelly's house, though, was the peace, love and kindness I found there. It was always pleasant to be with Shelly, and Mr. and Mrs. Martin treated me with tenderness, like one of their own.

When I was ten, Mrs. Martin taught me how to swim. She always had a word of praise or encouragement for me. Once she took me aside and asked me about the bruises on my body. She made me look her straight in the eye. I tried to squirm away, but she firmly held both of my arms. So I looked her straight in the eye and told her a lie: "I fall down a lot. I run into things." She knew I was lying, but what could she do? "If you ever want to talk about it, you can come to me," she told me. I couldn't get away fast enough.

Of all the adults and teachers with whom I had contact throughout my childhood, Mrs. Martin was the only one who cared enough to inquire about what must have been obvious to many. If only I could have confided the truth to her, what a comforter she might have been. But then I might never have turned to the eternal Comforter and Lover of my soul.

By the time we were sophomores in high school, I began to notice a "cooling off" between Shelly and me. She was making new friends with other wealthy kids, and I was being left in the dust. By mid-term, she had stopped inviting me to her home, and she was ignoring me at school. I was deeply hurt but accepted it as what I deserved. I had always known we were from two different worlds and had wondered how she could have liked me to begin with.

Still, I longed for our old friendship, and one day I got up the courage to approach Shelly and ask her what happened to change her feelings toward me. I was floored by her response.

"You always came to my house," she said. "In all those years you never once invited me to your house. I don't think you liked me at all. You just wanted to swim in my pool."

To be misunderstood that completely is a pain akin to nothing else I know. Yet what else could she have thought? It was true. I had never invited her to my house. I was too ashamed to let her see the filth and drunkenness, cursing, fighting and abuse there. When we parted that day, our friendship was over. I had lost my best—my only—friend. I was overwhelmed with grief, and once again, I thought I faced life alone.

The sorrows, burdens and rejection of my young life began to exact a toll. By the time I was 16, I had started down the ravaging path of self-destruction. This was the most difficult period of my life.

I wish I could remember what I was thinking during the episodes of self-abuse I am about to describe, but I cannot. I know that I generally felt dirty, worthless and hopeless. I saw no purpose in my life whatsoever. These emotions triggered my aberrant behavior.

For at least a year, there were times when I would go off by myself (to the school rest room, church rest room, backyard, etc.), sit in a secluded corner and cut myself—usually on the arms and legs—with razor blades. I was not trying to commit suicide—the thought did not cross my mind. But I was filled with such self-hatred that I derived a morbid pleasure from causing myself injury and pain.

I do not remember how many times I did this, but I

have a number of scars remaining on my arms and legs today. They constantly remind me of all from which God has delivered me.

How well I can relate to the man described in Mark 5:1–20! He was a man with an unclean spirit—a madman, if you will—who wandered about crying and cutting himself with stones. (I have often wondered what caused his pain.) One day he saw Jesus afar off. That was the beginning of the end of his troubles. Jesus drove out the demons and gave him full deliverance. Then He assigned him a task: "Go home to your family and tell them how much the Lord has done for you, and how he has had mercy on you" (v. 20).

Who can more effectively describe God's deliverance than the one who has been delivered? If God can heal this demonic man (and me), He can heal anyone.

My healing was not to take place for several years, however. When I turned 17, my emotional instability began to take on a new twist, a twist that nearly proved fatal. Although the malady to which I would succumb is considered to be a 20th century phenomenon, I am reminded of Solomon's words: "Is there anything of which one can say, 'Look! This is something new'? It was here already, long ago; it was here before our time" (Ecc. 1:10).

I believe anorexia nervosa is at least as old as the days of the psalmist: "Some became fools through their rebellious ways and suffered affliction because of their iniquities. They loathed all food and drew near the gates of death" (Ps. 107:17–18).

In all the medical books I have reviewed, I have never read a better description of an eating disorder than the above. Nor have I seen a more effective cure, for the psalmist goes on to say: "Then they cried to the LORD in their trouble, and he saved them from their distress. He sent forth his word and healed them; he rescued them from the grave" (vv. 19-20).

At 5' 5" and 115 pounds, I thought I was a little too fat. During the summer before my senior year in high school, I decided I needed to lose 5 pounds. I took them off with ease and then decided I should lose 5 more. By the time school started in September, I weighed about 100 pounds. I had no idea of the trouble I was in. I felt good and liked being thin, but I really didn't think I was thin enough. Actually, I thought I was still fat.

At school, everyone seemed to notice that I had lost weight. This was all the reinforcement I needed, because in the past no one had noticed me at all. Dieting became an absolute obsession.

I had never heard of anorexia nervosa, and apparently none of the doctors who would later treat me had either. (In 1968 the disorder was not publicized as it is today.) I can testify to its hideous, unyielding grasp on a young victim's mind. It was one of the most horrifying things that has ever happened to me. I was not horrified at the time, however—only driven. I was driven to make straight A's, driven to be good, driven to starve.

Not eating at home was easy. When I left for school with an empty stomach, my mother was still asleep. When I returned home from school, she was drunk. No one cooked meals, and we never ate together. Sometimes I would prepare soup or a sandwich for my father. Many times he stopped at a grill for his supper. I always told him that I had eaten earlier and wasn't hungry. He always accepted that. I was starving to death before my parents' eyes, and they never noticed.

What did I think was happening? Did I realize my behavior was markedly abnormal? I don't remember. I knew only that I *had* to keep losing weight, and each day I grew thinner.

I was existing on about 300 calories a day—some days less. I began to have difficulty concentrating. I tried desperately to study, but I was unable to comprehend what I was reading. Sometimes it would take an hour to read and understand one paragraph. Yet I did not relate this problem to my dieting at all. Nor did I associate the self-induced starvation with my thinning, fuzzy hair or the cessation of my period. My body was beginning to shut down.

I continued to attend school everyday. By the end of October, I weighed 70 pounds. But I still was unsatisfied and desired to lose more.

Then one Friday I collapsed at school and was taken to the hospital. When I regained consciousness, I was surrounded by medical personnel who were drawing vials of blood, taking an EKG and asking a myriad of questions. Since anorexia nervosa was not a commonly known disorder at that time, the doctors believed me when I told them I had a healthy appetite and was eating normally. Since the preliminary blood work indicated metabolic acidosis, the initial diagnosis was uncontrolled diabetes mellitus.

As I lay in the hospital for the next two weeks, I continued to starve myself. When my meals were brought to me, I pretended to eat and then flushed the food down the toilet. I was in the clasp of a demonic illness, and I could not shake myself free.

Further tests did not confirm the diagnosis of diabetes,

and no other diagnosis surfaced. The hospital medical staff and my private physician were convinced that my problem was either endocrinologic or carcinomatoid but were unable to verify either diagnosis. They decided to send me to the Medical College of Virginia. But a bed was not available, so I was placed on a waiting list.

The entire time I was in the hospital, I was never fed intravenously. The reason behind this, I am sure, is that the infusion of sodium chloride and/or glucose solution would skew the results of blood work and make a diagnosis more difficult to ascertain. So I continued to emaciate and came, I believe, to the point of death. During those days of waiting for a bed at the medical school, a great battle was waged in the spirit world over my sinful soul.

"But the eyes of the LORD are on those who fear him, on those whose hope is in his unfailing love, to deliver them from death and keep them alive in famine" (Ps. 33:18–19).

According to most of the information available on anorexia nervosa today, it is a serious psychological illness with a shaky prognosis, even when the patient is given psychiatric care. Without therapy, it is considered hopeless. Many girls, even after overcoming the eating disorder, die later as a result of damage incurred by the heart and other vital organs during starvation. At the very least, they are left barren.

But mine is a story with a different, happier ending than most, for Jesus came—the Great Physician, *Jehovah-ropheka.* I did not yet know Him. He was a stranger to me, and there was no one to introduce us. But He came.

I was awakened in the middle of the night by a strong desire for food. I not only wanted to eat for the first time in months—I *had* to eat. The next morning I began eating again. I ate lightly at first because I was quickly filled, but I began gaining weight right away. The weight gain didn't bother me—a sure sign that I was healed.

The doctors could not understand why I was improving and gaining weight, but they rejoiced and put my transfer to the medical college hospital on hold. I continued to gain weight every day and was released from the hospital when I weighed 80 pounds. Never again was I troubled with an eating disorder. I was cured of a disease I did not understand by a Physician I did not know.

Could it be that God had a purpose for my life, that my existence was not a mistake after all? Yes! There are no mistakes—only a marvelous, foreordained plan. I didn't see it yet, but I would.

Jesus, I Come

Out of my bondage, sorrow and night,
Jesus, I come, Jesus I come;
Into Thy freedom, gladness and light,
Jesus, I come to Thee.
Out of my sickness into Thy health,
Out of my want and into Thy wealth,
Out of my sin and into Thyself,
Jesus, I come to thee.

Out of my shameful failure and loss,
Jesus I come, Jesus I come;
Into the glorious gain of Thy cross,
Jesus I come to Thee.
Out of earth's sorrows into Thy balm,
Out of life's storms and into Thy calm,
Out of distress to jubilant psalm,
Jesus, I come to Thee.

—William T. Sleeper

Chapter 10

The First Day of Life

Returning home from the hospital would have been difficult at any time. I was still very weak and too tired to face conflict. But it was Christmastime, which made matters worse.

In *The Screwtape Letters,* C. S. Lewis wrote, "Men are not angered by mere misfortune but by misfortune conceived as injury. And the sense of injury depends on the feeling that a legitimate claim has been denied." He goes on to describe how Satan gains a foothold when a person believes that those things he desires and for which he longs (but is denied) are "in some mysterious sense, his personal birthright."

This explains why holidays are so much more difficult than ordinary days when spent in any type of suffering or pain. If at no other time, don't we deserve to be happy at Christmas? Or on our birthday or anniversary? Satan would have us think so. For at the moment we begin to believe we have a right to something that we have been denied, we become miserable, despondent and angry.

God blessed me at an early age with an attitude of acceptance of my lot in life. I do not remember ever feeling that I was deserving of a different home or different parents or a better life. Yes, I longed for them, especially for a mother who would love me. But I never believed that I had a *right* to them. I recognized early that there are few disappointments for the little girl who expects nothing.

However, Christmas was another story. As I grew older, I observed the great celebrations other families enjoyed. This made the drunkenness and abuse that accompanied Christmas at my house increasingly hard to bear. The heartaches of everyday life were intensified during the holidays. I despised and feared what were for me black, pain-filled days, which others seemed to await with joyous expectation. Somehow, the message of "peace on earth, goodwill toward men" never made it to my house.

The Christmas after I was released from the hospital was especially difficult. My mother was surlier than ever. Her sarcastic tongue was her most menacing weapon, and with it she spewed forth hostility and venom. She had grown comfortable with my absence during the six weeks I was hospitalized and now was having to adjust to my presence again.

I can't know this for sure, but I must have looked exactly like my biological father. (I certainly didn't resemble anyone else in my family.) What a reproach I must have been to Mother every time she looked at me. And she did not hide her hatred for me—it was evident in her facial expressions, her words and her behavior. Etched forever in my memory is the disgust on her face whenever she looked at me.

Although I was well on the road to recovery, by January it was obvious that I would not be able to return to school that year. Consequently, I would not graduate with my class. It seems strange now, but this did not bother me very much. Compared with the rest of my life, it was not an overwhelming problem.

As soon as I regained enough strength, I began walking to the library nearly every day. There I spent my time reading and studying, avoiding time at home.

The next September I began my senior year again with a new set of classmates and a resolve to do better than my best.

I graduated the following June with a 4.0 average and no plans for my future. I knew there was no money for college, and I did not feel qualified to go in spite of my excellent performance in high school. Straight A's don't overcome a lifetime of being called "stupid" and "worthless." I felt that I would never do anything worthwhile.

After my stay in the hospital the previous year, I had pondered the possibility of becoming a nurse. Many of the nurses with whom I had contact were cold and indifferent—just doing a job. But one had been different. I remember her well. She had carrot-colored hair, very round proportions and a genuine, caring smile. She worked the night shift and always came in for a visit after some of her routine duties were accomplished. I looked forward to her visits each night.

She tried to make me comfortable with extra pillows (it's hard to lie comfortably in bed when there is nothing between your skin and your bones) and even brought me snacks from her own lunch—which I promptly discarded when she left. She made me feel cared for in a way I never had before. And she caused a longing to develop within me—a desire to be a nurse just like her, to make someone else feel cared for and comforted.

When I mentioned this to my mother later, she hooted, "You! A nurse?! What a joke! You don't have what it takes to be a nurse! You'll never amount to anything, you filthy cur!"

I wouldn't have become a nurse apart from the grace of my compassionate Lord. The next event He placed in my life led to the fulfillment of my dream and, eventually, to the life I know today.

A couple who attended the same Methodist church I had attended all those years needed a nanny. Childless for 11 years, they had recently adopted a baby girl and then conceived another baby. After a difficult pregnancy and delivery, the mother needed help with her two little ones. I was astonished when they asked me. *Didn't they know I could do nothing right? How could they possibly think I was capable of caring for their babies?*

I didn't know the answers to those questions, and I didn't care. Newly graduated with no plans, I was thrilled to have a place to go and something to do. And I dearly loved children. So I agreed to be a nanny at least for the summer, and I was completely moved into their house by the end of June 1970.

During my stay there I learned many invaluable lessons about child care, about the functioning of a normal, happy family and about the joy of self-sacrifice. I was given room and board and $20 a week. But more than that, I was given encouragement and a new hope for my future.

I lived with that family for 14 months. After learning of my dream to become a nurse, they convinced me that I should try. They even procured the necessary applications to Portsmouth General Hospital School of Nursing. I seriously doubted that I would be accepted. But I was, and in September 1971, I embarked on a new, exciting adventure.

My first two years in nursing school were a blur of activity. All of my hard study in high school paid off: I had good study habits and did not find the courses inordinately difficult, the way some of the girls did. (One-third of my class dropped out the first year.) We took basic academic courses—English, chemistry, sociology, psychology, anatomy and physiology—at Old Dominion University. Our nursing courses were taught on the hospital campus, and, of course, we did our clinical training in the hospital. I supported myself by working as a nurse's aide some evenings and nearly all weekends. The rest of the time I studied. There was little time for sleep. I loved all the busyness, though, and thrived on my rigorous schedule.

The manner in which my education was financed is still a source of wonder to me. God provided for me in a marvelous, mystifying way.

The first week of school, Mrs. Paulsen,* the school's director, called me into her office to discuss my tuition. I had saved enough money for my books and uniforms—that was all. I had no tuition money. "How were you planning to pay for your education?" she asked me. "I don't know," I replied. *I might as well start packing*, I thought. "How about your parents? Can't they pay?" "Oh, no! Don't call my parents," I responded. "They don't have any money, and they don't think I'll make a nurse anyway."

Mrs. Paulsen gazed at me with furrowed brows as I fidgeted in my seat. I felt immensely stupid for being there with no money, and I wanted to escape. After what seemed to me to be hours, her expression melted into almost a smile. "Well," she said, "we'll have to see what can be done." She dismissed me from her office with a wave of her hand.

---

*name has been changed

A few weeks later she stopped me in the hallway and said, "Don't worry about your tuition this year. Someone thinks you *will* make a nurse. Now prove that someone to be right."

Every year until my senior year she told me the same thing. That year the alumni association gave me a scholarship—a full year's tuition.

Tears roll down my face even now as I remember it. I did not pay one cent for my education. My Father paid it all. "The LORD has done this, and it is marvelous in our eyes" (Ps. 118:23).

I loved nursing. It was rewarding and fulfilling, and I should have been immeasurably happy. But by the end of my junior year, some ominous clouds were rolling back into my life.

I cannot describe how difficult it is to become disentangled from an abusive past. Often there are attitudes and thought processes that remain intact in spite of an intense effort to eradicate them.

As much as I longed to break away from my past, I remained in close contact with my mother during my college years. Not once did she call or write me, and I didn't visit home; but I called frequently, always talking to Mother because my father never answered the phone. (Mother ruled the house and the phone. She screened the mail, too, so there was little chance of communicating with Daddy.)

Conversations with Mother were always painful and occasionally heated. Sometimes I was so wounded and angry I would vow never to call back. But I always felt remorseful and gave in, calling her again within a day or two.

Trying to make pleasant conversation and desperate to make her proud of me, I would tell Mother about dorm life, my grades and my accomplishments in clinical training. My news was always met with a stony silence—after which she would talk about something totally unrelated, as if she hadn't heard me—or with a mocking grunt or a prophecy of doom.

"It's going to get much harder. You don't know anything yet—just wait and see. You'll never make it."

Sometimes she would give credence to her prediction by telling me she had talked to "others" who agreed that I would never succeed. This angered me, but I was also afraid that she might be right.

Discouragement stalked me. I knew better than to listen to her tales and believe her anonymous naysayers, but self-doubt refused to relinquish any control to reason.

Suppose I do fail? What then? The thought of failure sickened me. *I'll have to work harder* was the delusion under which I continued to labor. *I must succeed at any cost.*

Because of my heavy work schedule and long hours of study, I fell into a state of exhaustion. I longed for sleep but allowed little time for it—no more than three or four hours a night.

When I did sleep, I had nightmares. I began dreaming that my father came into my room under cover of darkness, placed one hand over my mouth and with his other hand began to undress me. I would awaken, terrified, in a cold sweat and with my heart pounding. It would take several minutes for me to distinguish the dream from reality. Then I would be too frightened to go back to sleep. This happened over and over again. Sleep became my enemy.

I found no time for recreation. All the other girls went home on weekends and holidays, but where could I go? I stayed in the dormitory alone and worked as an aide at the hospital. This began to depress me. I felt abandoned, alone and forsaken. My solitude magnified the lack of love in my life.

My senior year was full of pain, and my depression deepened. Most of the other girls had already married or had marriage plans. I wasn't even dating—had rarely ever dated. *No one could ever want me*, I thought. *I'll never be married, never have the children I long for. My life has no purpose at all. I would be better off dead.* I not only thought that, I believed it with all my heart. Ending my life appeared to be the perfect solution to all of my problems, nightmares and pain.

In those days, when hospitalization insurance companies had less control over hospital policy, many hospital practices were extremely wasteful. For example, when a patient was discharged from the hospital, the remaining medications in his box were thrown away. (Now they are carefully accounted for, sent back to the pharmacy and credited to his account.) This made it easy for me to begin hoarding the tranquilizers with which I planned to overdose myself. When my patients went home, I sorted through the leftover medications and kept the ones I wanted (mainly phenobarbitol and various sleeping pills), throwing the rest away. I had no intention of doing a halfway job. I needed plenty of pills. In about three months I had more than enough.

It was a very cold Friday in late January. Another miserable Christmas had come and gone. I was overwhelmed with grief. *I'm not spending one more lonely weekend in this dorm,* I thought. I took the Ziploc bag of tablets and capsules out of my dresser drawer, emptied it onto my bed and counted my colorful collection. I do not remember how many pills there were, but I was satisfied that there were plenty. I scooped them all back into the bag and hid it in the drawer under my clothes. *Tonight is the night,* I calmly, almost happily, decided. I had not signed up to work that weekend, so no one would look for me until Monday. I raced off to what I thought would be my last day of school and work and life.

When my clinical duties were finished for the day, I took my usual route back to the dorm, which led through the hospital lobby. A brochure on one of the tables caught my eye as I passed. *What were those things?* I had noticed them here and there about the hospital but had never been curious enough to read one. That day, however, I felt strangely compelled to go back and pick one up. As though moved by an outside force, I made my way back to the table. *This is silly,* I thought, and I looked around the room to be sure no one was watching me.

The front of the brochure pictured a cross and an open Bible. It read, "God's Four Steps to Salvation." *Oh,* I thought, *religious propaganda. I've tried religion, and it doesn't work.* I started to toss it away but again felt a strong compulsion to keep it. I slid it inconspicuously between my books and carried it to my room. *It couldn't hurt to read something religious before I die,* I reasoned.

I like to imagine the grief this must have caused Satan. My soul was dangling over hell by a single thread. I was to be his that night. Then an angel, as it were, placed a Gospel tract in my hand.

Shortly after I returned to my room, the other girls

cleared out for the weekend, and it was quiet. I pulled the tract out of my books and began to read.

The first thing the brochure said was that God loves me and desires an abundant life for me. It quoted John 3:16 ("For God so loved the world that he gave his one and only Son, that whoever believes in him shall not perish but have eternal life"); John 10:10 ("I have come that they may have life, and have it to the full"); and John 11:25 ("I am the resurrection and the life. He who believes in me will live, even though he dies"). *Funny, I thought, if God is God and He wants me to be happy and to experience joy and peace, why can't He just give them to me?*

As I continued reading, my question was answered. I saw that I could not be happy and at peace because God is holy and my sin separates me from Him. Romans 3:23 ("all have sinned and fall short of the glory of God") and 6:23 ("the wages of sin is death") were quoted. I immediately recognized the truth of these verses. I knew I was a sinner. I had always felt distant from God, even when I had tried so desperately to reach Him through prayer and church attendance.

The tract further explained that if I remained in my sin, trying to bridge the gap between God and myself through my efforts (good works, religion, morality, etc.), I would remain separated from Him in hell, forever. *But what can I possibly do?*

Step three made the answer plain. I saw that there was only one solution to my dilemma. God had given His only Son, Jesus Christ, to die for my sins.

That sacrifice on Calvary's cross had bridged the gap and made it possible for me to receive forgiveness, peace, abundant life and eternal life.

I had heard of Jesus all my life, but His death on the cross had never seemed relevant. *What did the old, rugged cross have to do with my sin? Wasn't it just wicked men murdering a good man?* But now it all came together perfectly like pieces of a puzzle. *It was* my sin *that put the Lord Jesus on that cross.*

I could hardly read step four fast enough. There I saw that I must trust in Christ's sacrifice as the only means of forgiveness from my sin. I needed to receive the gift that God had so freely given. *Can it possibly be this simple? Is this really God's way?*

The words of many old hymns I had learned as a child came flooding back to me. I realized that they confirmed all of the things I had been reading. *Of course! Why hadn't I seen it before? Did everyone in the world know about this but me?*

The back of the tract contained a suggested prayer. I decided to use it because I wanted to do everything just right, and I feared that if I used my own words it might not "work."

Blinded with tears, I slid off the bed and knelt beside it. "Dear Heavenly Father," I prayed, "I realize that I am a sinner and, believing that Christ died for my sins, I here and now trust Him to be my personal Savior, to forgive all my sins, to change my heart and give me everlasting life as He promised to do. I now invite the Lord Jesus Christ to come into my heart and life as my Savior. I promise to follow Him as Lord of my life."

I had knelt down in grave clothes, but I stood up in robes of righteousness—the righteousness of Christ. There was no preacher in that room with me, no counselor or teacher. But the Holy Spirit was there, instructing me that

I was a new creature, that the old things of my life were passed away and all things were new (2 Cor. 5:17). In my heart I knew that I belonged to Someone now and that He was mine—forever.

In heaven, the angels were rejoicing, and in that tiny dormitory room, I slept a long, peaceful sleep.

> No condemnation now I dread,
> I am my Lord's and He is mine;
> Alive in Him, my living Head,
> And clothed in righteousness divine.
>
> Amazing love! How can it be
> That Thou, my God, shouldst die for me!
>
> —Charles Wesley

Like a River Glorious

Like a river glorious is God's perfect peace,
Over all victorious in its bright increase;
Perfect, yet it floweth fuller ev'ry day,
Perfect, yet it groweth deeper all the way.

. . . . . .

Ev'ry joy or trial falleth from above,
Traced upon our dial by the Sun of Love;
We may trust Him fully all for us to do—
They who trust Him wholly find Him wholly true.

Stayed upon Jehovah, hearts are fully blest—
Finding, as He promised, perfect peace and rest.

—Francis R. Havergal

Chapter 11

Nothing Shall Offend

"I love the LORD, for he heard my voice;
he heard my cry for mercy. Because he turned his
ear to me, I will call on him as long as I live.

"The cords of death entangled me, the anguish of the grave
came upon me; I was overcome by trouble and sorrow.
Then I called on the name of the LORD:
'O LORD, save me!'

"The LORD is gracious and righteous; our God is
full of compassion. The LORD protects the simplehearted;
when I was in great need, he saved me.

"Be at rest once more, O my soul,
for the LORD has been good to you.

"For you, O LORD, have delivered my soul from death,
my eyes from tears, my feet from stumbling,
that I may walk before the LORD in the land
of the living" (Ps. 116:1–9).

What joy! What peace! I had never known life could be so hopeful and wonderful. I was a newborn babe, with the thrill of a new life before me and so much to learn.

As soon as I came to Christ for salvation, I had an

insatiable desire to know Him better, to learn all I could about Him. So I knew that I must have a Bible. The next day, a bright, cold Saturday, I took the bus to town and bought one, devouring it on the trip back to the hospital as a starving man would consume a meal.

The words of Scripture danced on the pages. Every verse I read held profound meaning for me. What a contrast to my earlier attempts at reading the Bible. Then, I was hardly able to understand a word of it.

That Sunday, with all the excitement of a child on Christmas morning, I boarded a bus and headed back to the little church I had attended throughout my youth. I read my Bible all the way, anticipating the joy with which I would tell everyone about my experience. I didn't know I was "saved." In fact, I didn't know any of the Christian terminology. But I knew that something vast and deep had happened to me and that it had everything to do with Jesus Christ. I couldn't wait to tell them.

But they could certainly wait to hear. I was met with blank faces or quizzical expressions. I told them one by one and in small groups that I had asked Jesus to forgive my sins and that He had changed me and made me a new person. These were their responses:

"Yes, dear. We should ask Him to forgive us everyday."

"Oh, Glenda, you always were the most religious little thing."

"You had better watch out—you'll become a fanatic!"

How could I make them understand? This wasn't religion—this was the Lord Jesus.

For weeks I tried to explain salvation to the people in that church. One Sunday I brought in the Gospel tract that had revealed the truth to me. "Read this," I told them. "It will explain it all to you."

"Glenda, you aren't being misled by this stuff, are you? We don't believe this way in our church. God wouldn't send you to hell. He is loving and kind. We are all doing the best we can, and He understands that. What kind of God would send someone to hell?"

A pure and holy God, I thought, *or why did Jesus have to die?*

I went from believing I was the only person in the world who didn't know about God's plan of salvation to wondering if I were the only one who *did* know.

Someone else had to know, I thought, *or how did the tract get printed? That was it!* On the front of the tract was the name and telephone number of a church: Faith Baptist Church, Chesapeake, Virginia. I nervously dialed the number and explained to the voice on the other end what had happened to me. Right away she understood. "Just a minute," she said. "Let me get the pastor for you."

After introducing himself to me, the pastor asked me to explain to him, from the beginning, what had happened to me. The best I could, I told him about the Gospel tract I had read, how I knew it was true and that I had prayed the prayer on the back, asking Jesus Christ to forgive my sins and become Lord of my life. He was obviously delighted.

"Do you attend church anywhere?" he asked.

I explained to him about my little church. "They don't know about Jesus there," I said. "At least, not the way I know Him. I've been trying to tell them, but I just can't make them understand."

The pastor told me that I had done the right thing to

witness to them, but that I needed to be in a church where the Bible was preached so I could know more about Christ and become a better witness for Him.

This sounded right, but I was hesitant. *How can I leave people whom I have known and loved for so long? Who will tell them if I don't?*

The pastor perceived my uncertainty. "There are many good churches in our area. I'll be glad to give you a list of them so you'll know I'm not just trying to get you into my church."

"Well . . ."

"Listen to me. What would happen if you placed a burning match into a bucket of ice cubes?" he asked urgently.

I immediately visualized the smoking remains of a match in the midst of the still-frozen cubes. "The flame would go out, of course."

"That's exactly right. And right now you are like a little flame. You are on fire for God, but if you stay in a cold, dead church, you will never learn to burn brightly for the Lord, and your flame may even go out. Then you will be useless to God."

Useless? Now that struck a cord. Hadn't I always been useless? I belonged to God now. I couldn't bear being useless to Him. *I can't let that happen. I'll try this new church, at least for a while.*

Once again, God was guiding my every footstep. Members of Faith Baptist began picking me up every Sunday and Wednesday for services. Never mind that it was 30 miles out of their way. They loved the Lord in an exciting, vibrant way, and it was evident in everything they said and did. And they loved me too.

The sermons were like none I had ever heard before—clear, direct, powerful. Everything was based on Scripture. I began meditating on God's Word day and night. It was more important to me than eating.

In March of that same year (1975), I was baptized. I committed myself to follow God anywhere, to do anything, if only He would guide me.

God gave me a love for truth, and I renounced the deceitfulness that had always been a part of my life. As I drew nearer to Him, I became more aware of my sinfulness. But my new church taught me well, so I knew I had only to bring all my sin to the cross and leave it there. The contentment that had for so long eluded me was mine.

But one thing still clouded my joy. The closer I drew to the Lord, the blacker my past appeared to me. What should have been easier for me to face became more difficult. I saw what had been done to me through different eyes, and it seemed worse than it had before. *How could my parents have done those horrible things to me? I was just a little girl. Why didn't they let me be a little girl?* I had been beaten, stripped, molested, cursed, screamed at, kicked and hated when all I ever wanted was love. I would have done anything for their love. Now I hated them for all they had done to me. I didn't want to hate them, but I couldn't help it.

Then one day as I was reading Psalm 119, I came across a verse that spoke directly to me: "Great peace have they who love thy law and nothing shall offend them" (v. 165, NKJV). *Nothing, Lord? Nothing? Not anything? Not even the desecration of an innocent? The profaning of a childhood?* ". . . and nothing shall offend."

"Oh, God," I prayed, "if it displeases You for me to be offended, then somehow take it from me. Tear the resentment out of me. I long to be Yours wholly and completely. I want to forgive those who have offended me as You forgave me of all my offenses. I know I can't do it, Lord, but I am willing to do it. I choose to do it. Now help me, Father, for Jesus' sake."

God did a marvelous thing that day. He wrought forgiveness in my heart, which I never could have placed there. He showed me Calvary once more, but in a clearer, more personal way than when I had come for salvation. I saw the horror of my sin, nailing the Son of God to that miserable cross, torturing Him, mocking Him, spitting on Him. Yet He had forgiven me freely. No one had committed such atrocities against me. How could I do anything less than forgive?

Forgiveness came. And with it came healing, complete peace and freedom—absolute freedom—to serve my God and to enjoy His love and peace now and forevermore.

I grew to love my parents, and, though they were never able to return that love, they ceased scoffing at and showing disdain for my Savior. And eventually God gave me the freedom to go to them and ask forgiveness for my poor attitude and lack of respect for them while I was growing up. Only God could have done that. And only He could have given me the peace that followed.

He Hideth My Soul

A wonderful Savior is Jesus my Lord,
A wonderful Savior to me;
He hideth my soul in the cleft of the rock,
Where rivers of pleasure I see.

A wonderful Savior is Jesus my Lord—
He taketh my burden away;
He holdeth me up and I shall not be moved,
He giveth me strength as my day.

With numberless blessings each moment He crowns
And, filled with His fullness divine,
I sing in my rapture, "O Glory to God
For such a Redeemer as mine!"

He hideth my soul in the cleft of the rock
That shadows a dry, thirsty land;
He hideth my life in the depths of His love
And covers me there with His hand.

—Fanny J. Crosby

Chapter 12

River of Pleasures

"How precious is Your lovingkindness, O God!
Therefore the children of men put their trust under the
shadow of Your wings. They are abundantly satisfied
with the fullness of Your house, and You give them
drink from the river of Your pleasures"(Ps. 36:7–8, NKJV).

On May 23, 1975, I graduated from nursing
school. Much had transpired since I entered
that school just a few years before. I had passed from death
unto life. I, who had been illegitimate, now had a goodly
heritage. I was not fatherless anymore, but enjoyed the
lovingkindness of my Heavenly Father. No longer did I
carry a burden of sin. I was free to drink of the swollen
river of His pleasures.

I thought my joy was full, but who can restrain the
gracious goodness of our God? Who can hold Him to the
expected or even the desired? He began to unfold before
me a life for which I had never dared dream.

God had someone waiting for me at Faith Baptist
Church—the dearest, kindest, most godly and gentlemanly
bachelor in the world—David Lawrence Revell. Quiet.
Reserved. Twenty-eight years old. Six-feet, one-inch tall.
Thin. Piercing blue eyes. Sandy hair. Sharply chiseled fea-
tures. *Wouldn't he make the perfect Bob Cratchit?* I mused
when we were introduced.

We met on a Wednesday night at prayer meeting. It

was the night before my state board examinations began. I knew I needed to get back to the dorm early and rest (I was renting a room in the dorm that summer for $50 a month until the new class came that September), but I consented to his invitation to go out for a bite to eat after church. It turned out to be an unusual and comical first date.

Both of us ordered spaghetti, but we did more talking than eating. It was fun getting to know this soft-spoken man.

After a final cup of coffee we decided to go. David picked up the check and reached into his pocket. He shifted in his chair and reached into another pocket. He did this three or four times. He slapped his shirt pocket, stood up, sat down, looked around on the floor and dug into his pants pockets again. I tried to look as if I didn't notice. He continued this for a few more moments. His face blanched, and he sat down heavily in his chair.

"Is something the matter?" I asked, no longer able to contain the question.

"I don't have my wallet." The words formed on his lips but were unaccompanied by sound. He cleared his throat and tried again. "I can't find my wallet. I must have left it at home." The color returned to his face, then drained again.

This guy must be quite a character. This is kind of funny, though. I wonder if I have any money with me.

I checked my purse and found that I had enough money to cover the meal and the tip. "It's OK," I said. "I have enough."

With much apology, David took my money, assuring me repeatedly that he would pay me back right away.

Sure you will, I thought.

As David drove me to the dorm, he told me a few more things about himself. He had recently bought a small house and was busy fixing it up as a "bachelor's pad." He had lived in a mobile home for several years and had decided a house would be a better investment.

Although I had enjoyed our evening together, I started feeling distracted by anxiety over the state board exams I would face the next two days. *Should I try to study, or should I just go to bed and get a good night's sleep?* I was lost in my thoughts when I suddenly realized we were not heading in the direction of the hospital.

"I don't think we can get to the dorm this way," I quickly told him, wondering what he was up to.

"Oh, I know we can't. I'm taking you by my house first so I can give back your money."

My internal alarm squealed and clanged. "I'm not going in your house!"

I was honestly afraid. My experience told me that men could not be trusted. This didn't look good at all. I wanted to get out of the car.

David pulled into his driveway. Smiling at me, he said, "I don't want you to go in my house. You wait right here. I'll only be a minute."

I watched him walk up the sidewalk, fumble with his keys and enter the house. A light came on. I saw him pass by a front window. Gradually, I began to relax. My heart stopped pounding. I knew I had overreacted. As I thought over the events of the evening, the entire situation started to look hilarious.

I leaned back in the seat and waited for David to

return. A streetlight dimly illuminated the neat, little brick house—his bachelor's pad.

David couldn't have known that his bachelor status wouldn't survive another year. I couldn't have known that before me stood what would become the first home I would ever call my own, where David and I would begin our love-filled life together.

But God is never caught by surprise. Before He spoke the world into existence, He had planned it all.

"The plans of the LORD stand firm forever, the purposes of his heart through all generations" (Ps. 33:11).

Hurrying back to the car, David paid off his debt, then drove me home. He was a perfect gentleman, and I was relieved.

He now says he fell in love with me that night. Although I can't say I was in love with him then, I did hope to hear from him again.

I did. The next day he surprised me by showing up for lunch at the Holiday Inn in Norfolk, where I was taking the all-important exams. We talked and ate together. It was a pleasant respite to my grueling day.

As the remaining weeks of that summer unfolded, my world changed rapidly. Everything seemed to fly in a hundred happy directions. I passed the state boards and became a registered nurse. Wow! I had to pinch myself to make sure I wasn't dreaming.

The dorm room I was renting was available only until September 1, when I would have to leave to make room for the incoming students. Where would I go? The closest apartment building was miles from the hospital, and I had no transportation. How would I get to work each day? My head swam with questions. This problem seemed insurmountable.

But God has no problems, and I was quickly learning that He could take care of me in every difficulty.

"Meet this need somehow, dear Father. Please show me what to do."

A young man in the church I attended had recently inherited a car from his father and therefore didn't need the '62 Chevrolet Bel-Air he had been driving.

"Would you like to have it?" he asked me. "It needs a little work."

"How much do you want for it?"

"Nothing. I'm giving it to you."

"Oh, thank you! Thank you so much!" I said in astonished gratitude. I had to pinch myself again.

Everyone should have a Father like mine, I thought. My heart leaped in praise to Him.

David did the required repairs and had the car running well in no time.

But there remained one problem—I didn't know how to drive.

"Don't worry. I'll teach you," David said.

He had only two weeks to teach me, because that was my deadline for moving. He had to start from the beginning, too, because I didn't even know how to "turn the thing on," as I told him.

Day after day, he patiently took me out driving, instructing me in seat belts and turn signals, parallel parking and right-of-way rules. It was a learning experience for both of us. He learned never to stomp on my foot, even if I didn't apply the brake as forcefully as he might like. I learned to avoid stressful situations with a man whose stomach is empty. Together, we learned to laugh at ourselves and to be agreeable in our disagreements.

Amazingly, we emerged from the driving lessons more drawn to one another than before. I was grateful to this kind, chivalrous man for giving me so much help. He was grateful, I think, that the ordeal was over and that, except for one knocked-down restaurant sign, the world was unscathed by it.

As soon as I received my driver's license, it was time to move. Once again, David helped me. He transported all my belongings from the dorm to the apartment. There wasn't much settling in to do—I didn't own any furniture. But that didn't bother me. I was free and independent and thankful to God for all He had accomplished for me in such a short time.

The first night in my apartment, I slept on a bed of folded blankets on the floor. As I lay there in the darkness listening to the creaks and groans of an unfamiliar building, my thoughts retraced the previous year: my depression and near-suicide, God's miraculous intervention resulting in my salvation, the new church family God had given me, my baptism, my deepening relationship with David, becoming a registered nurse, getting a car and my driver's license and moving into my own apartment.

I was overwhelmed with relief and gratitude. Jubilant tears flowed as I quietly worshiped my Heavenly Father. I sensed His nearness. Words I had recently heard in a sermon about Job came to mind: "Though he slay me, yet will I trust him" (Job 13:15). It felt as if God were somehow calling to me, asking for my unmitigated trust. *Though You slay me, yet will I trust You*, my heart whispered to my God, for I dearly loved Him. Love and surrender are easy companions. Then I sank into the contented sleep of a well-cared-for child.

The next morning I nervously drove to work for the first time. That old tank of a car had no power steering—no power anything—and was a bear to drive, but I considered it as comfortable and beautiful as a limousine. I loved it and the sense of freedom it gave me. I thought I had all the blessings I could contain—until I returned to my apartment that afternoon and found it completely furnished, with everything from sofas and chairs and a bed and dresser to dining room furniture and lamps. There were even pictures hanging on the walls! Pinch, pinch, pinch. This time, I *had* to be dreaming.

At first I thought I had barged in the wrong apartment—but, no, that was my number on the door, and my key had worked in the lock. I walked through the rooms over and over again, mouth agape, wondering how this could have happened. Even the bed was made with my sheets and blankets. It was unfathomable.

I understand God has promised to take care of me, but I had no idea He delivers furniture! I was sure God had dropped my new furniture right out of heaven and into my apartment. And in a sense, He did.

I soon learned that a dear saint in our church, who was the personnel manager of a local furniture chain, had procured the display furniture from one of their stores and arranged for it to be delivered and set up while I was at work. What unimaginable generosity!

Never will I forget that marvelous act of kindness.

God used it to strengthen my already expanding faith and to draw me more tightly into His loving arms. "For you make me glad by your deeds, O LORD; I sing for joy at the works of your hands" (Ps. 92:4).

Since graduation I had been working on a medical-surgical floor at the hospital, but at my request I was transferred to the OB-GYN floor. How I loved working with those mothers and babies! It was, most of the time, a cheerful, uplifting place to work. I decided to follow a career in that specialty.

David and I were seeing each other frequently, going out for meals and attending church services together. I saw in him the unusual mixture of tenderness, meekness and strength. I wondered why he had never had a serious relationship with any girl before and why he would want one with me. I could see he did, though, and it both scared and pleased me. Yes, his character appeared to be sterling, but I had learned years before that my judgment was not to be trusted. *Could any one really care for me? Is David just stringing me along, setting me up for the kill? Will he erode my guard with kindness and then violate me? Will he reject me? Would God let that happen?*

I struggled with these questions in those otherwise carefree days. I voiced my fears only to my loving Father and continued to timidly but carefully observe David's life. His attentiveness and kindness toward me melted my heart, but it was his devotion to God that most impressed me. I saw him earnestly seek God's will in everything. More and more, he earned my trust.

On Wednesday, October 13, 1975, David and I attended prayer meeting together, and afterwards he delivered me to my door. We usually said a brief good night and parted ways there, for we agreed from the outset that it would not look good for him to accompany me inside. We wanted to avoid any appearance of evil, and we certainly did not want to place ourselves in the way of temptation. Purity was important to us. Our Father demanded it. But this particular night, David lingered, making small talk and finally suggesting that we have a cup of coffee together.

"Do you think we should?" I asked skeptically.

"Just for a few minutes. I have a little something for you—it's in the car. I wanted to give it to you tonight."

"I just don't think it's a good idea," I said. "We agreed on that, remember?"

"It's important." David looked at me imploringly.

"Well, OK. But only for a few minutes."

I unlocked my apartment door and went in, busying myself with brewing a pot of coffee. David quickly returned from the car and presented me with a huge box of candy, a Whitman's sampler. *Mmmm . . .* He knew my weakness, all right. *This was important?* I smiled to myself. *Oh, well. It was a thoughtful gesture.*

I showed my delight by tearing off the cellophane wrapper and downing a chocolate-covered nut. David then placed the box on the dining room table and sat down, while I went into the kitchen, bringing back two steaming cups of coffee. I sat down at the table opposite David, and we talked and ate. My capacity for chocolates is nearly limitless, but I knew David did not possess much of a sweet tooth. That's why I was amazed at how much candy he put away that night. By the time I poured our second cup of coffee, even I was beginning to feel a little sugar-saturated. But he kept on urging me to "eat one more," and, fearful of hurting his feelings, I complied.

Finally, out of desperation, I suspect, he pointed to one of the pieces left and said, "Why don't you try that one?"

"OK." Inwardly, I groaned.

As I lifted the piece of candy out of the box, I immediately saw that there was something unusual about it. *This isn't just a piece of candy. It's a tiny box with a chocolate-covered lid.*

I glanced up at David in amazement. He was smiling.

"Go on," he urged. "Open it."

With trembling fingers I removed the lid. A small scrap of paper fell into my lap, revealing an exquisite diamond ring.

I gasped. Neither of us spoke. I retrieved the slip of paper, unfolded it and read what David had written: "I love you. Will you marry me?"

Suddenly I felt altogether numb and tingly, hot and cold. My ears were ringing. I blinked in disbelief, then read the proposal again. *Somebody wants me? After all these years, somebody really wants me?*

David slipped out of his chair and kneeled in front of me. "Well? Will you marry me?" He removed the ring from its box and held my left hand in his.

I was unable to speak.

"Glenda, will you marry me?"

"Yes! Yes, I will." He slid the ring on my finger.

We laughed and cried and embraced. Never had I dreamed of such happiness. It didn't seem real. It wasn't possible.

"How on earth did you get this ring into the box of candy?" I asked in amazement. "It was sealed."

With obvious enjoyment, David told me how he had carefully steamed the cellophane off with a tea kettle, then slid the box out and removed one piece of candy. Meanwhile, he melted a chocolate bar and spooned the semi-liquid on the ring box and let it harden. After placing the small box into the larger box, he worked the cellophane back on and resealed the end with a heated iron.

What kind of man is this who would go to such trouble for me? Make me worthy of him, Father. Teach me to be a good wife.

We set our wedding date for the following April, and the intervening months flew by. David and I spent our time together discussing weightier topics than before: Did we want children? Yes, if God would be so gracious to us. Would I continue to work? No, I would resign from my job when we married so we could adjust, from the start, to one income. We talked about child-rearing techniques and our commitment to each other. We prayed together. It was a time of love and spiritual growth and rich happiness.

Amid all the joy and excitement, however, one sorrow still pressed its weight into my heart. I was unable to tell David about my past. Oh, some things he knew—they couldn't be hidden. He had met my parents. He knew Mother had a drinking problem. It was obvious that their relationship was far from normal. We talked about those things. But the sexual abuse—I was far too ashamed to tell anyone, especially David. I didn't want to completely destroy my parents in his mind. Yet I was also ashamed to keep it from him, wondering if I were defrauding him in some way by withholding information about myself.

I also entertained private concerns about the wedding itself. A very simple ceremony with a few friends and family present had been planned. What if my mother should come drunk? What if my family refused to come at all? They certainly hadn't exuded enthusiasm at the news of my engagement. Mother's only comment was to my sister: "I feel so sorry for David. He's getting stuck with Glenda."

In spite of my fears, April 3, 1976, arrived, and David and I were married in the church where we had both come as babes in Christ and had met ten months before. We had made arrangements with the associate pastor of the church for him to give me away if my parents didn't come. But they did come. And my father gave me away.

God had given David to me and placed me in a new family of my own. Was there ever joy like this? "A father to the fatherless, a defender of widows, is God in his holy dwelling. God sets the lonely in families" (Ps. 68:5–6).

Married life was like heaven to me. I was needed. I belonged. My days were filled with cleaning, washing, cooking and planning for the day when I might be a mother. We knew that anorexia nervosa could have left me sterile, so we asked our dear Father to have His perfect will in our lives, and we clung to hope.

Though my life was happier than it had ever been before, there remained one great difficulty that seemed to threaten our contentment and the stability of our marriage: Sex was emotionally and physically agonizing for me. I should have anticipated such a problem, but I didn't. Since God had removed so many obstacles in my life, I had assumed He would quickly eliminate this one. I soon learned not to presume upon God, who always acts according to the wisdom of His own timetable and who at times allows sorrow to be His beloved child's chief companion.

Again and again I entreated the Father to help me overcome my sexual inhibitions, but the marriage bed continued to evoke terrifying, repulsive memories. I had not yet escaped the horrific bed of my childhood. This situation was made even more painful because I loved David so much and wanted desperately to please him. It also intensified my feelings of inadequacy and worthlessness and my fear of losing his love.

Where was God in this? Why had He carried me so far and then dropped me suddenly into this gloomy abyss? I had no answers. For a time, God was silent.

David was also searching for bearings. Since I had never revealed my whole past to him, he was unable to understand my aversion to lovemaking (I tried unsuccessfully to cover up my displeasure) and interpreted it as rejection. He wrestled with feelings of confusion and frustration.

Neither of us could see it at the time, but through those troublesome months, God was lovingly, tenderly emptying us of ourselves, teaching us individually and as a couple to trust Him in the dark places, the impossible situations, the seemingly useless trials. He was stripping us of our expectations and clothing us in the garments of patience and faith—the very coverings we would so need for the stormy days ahead of us.

In November 1976 and April 1977, our first two babies (three- and four-month gestated) were taken to heaven by God. Those were dark and difficult days. How we longed for a child! But we had already experienced enough of the tender mercies of the Lord to know that He deserved our absolute, unconditional trust. His hard lessons had not been wasted on us. Our Father's wise discipline yielded the fruit of peace and thankfulness. In our deep sorrow we were able to praise Him.

Gradually, God lifted from me the emotionally crippling effects of molestation. Over the years I told David about the sexual abuse I had endured. I began to respond to my patient and loving husband with the freedom and self-abandonment that God intended, and we emerged with a marriage cemented in self-sacrifice and unconditional love. What a gift from God!

Meanwhile, we discovered that our dear Father had been reserving His best for us. My grieving heart was soon full of joy; my empty arms filled to overflowing.

"He settles the barren woman in her home as a happy mother of children. Praise the LORD" (Ps. 113:9).

On March 3, 1978, our dream for a child was made manifest in a darling little girl, Charlotte Renee. My joy transcended all previous imaginings.

But just three weeks after her birth, I was confronted with the sorrowful news that my father had died. To the best of my knowledge, he was without Christ. David and I had witnessed to him many times, pleading with him to receive the free gift of salvation from the loving Savior, who had died for him. But my father would never admit he was a sinner. He saw no need in himself for a Savior. He rejected the Son of God.

I was crushed. But God never sends grief apart from grace, and in that dark hour of lament, His grace sustained me.

Then on December 19, 1979, precious Sarah Colleen

was given to our family—all ten pounds of her! What a Christmas gift!

Two perfect little girls—who could ask for more? Certainly not my obstetrician. He explained to me that my uterine wall had been as thin as paper when he delivered Sarah and could easily have ruptured, killing us both. "Two C-sections and two large babies—that's enough," my doctor said. "It would be too dangerous for you to have any more, OK?"

His warning seemed reasonable, and I took it to heart. But always, there was a tugging at my maternal heartstrings, an inner voice asking, "Are you sure God has no more babies for you?"

I prayed often for wisdom for David and me as we struggled to decide whether or not to have more children. We did not want to be foolish, yet we were even more hesitant to say no to God if He had more children planned for us.

After two years of seeking God's will, we felt confident that He wanted us to trust Him for my health and safety should He choose to bless us with another little one.

He did. On January 25, 1983, a delightful little boy, Jason Andrew, joined the crew. "A boy! What do you do with boys?" I laughed through tears of joy.

My knowledge of baby boys had greatly increased by 1985 when, on June 24, God gave us another treasure— Daniel Lindsay. He was plump and beautiful! I was in ecstasy and madly in love with our four children.

But one of my dreams lay broken and in ruins. My lifelong cry for a mother's love was muted forever. On June 19, five days before Daniel's birth, my mother died.

A year before she had made a profession of faith. I had witnessed to her (as often as I found her sober and lucid) for the ten years since my salvation experience. At first she mocked me and derided my faith. Not until I had come to her for forgiveness would she listen. It was then I began to notice her gradually softening toward the Lord. She remained bitter and hostile toward me, however, so I asked my pastor if he would speak with her about her need for Jesus. Mother agreed to visit with him—in itself a miracle—and that day she bowed her head and her heart to the Savior, asking Him for forgiveness and peace.

How I rejoiced over her redeemed soul! I was sure that this would change everything, enabling her to have a relationship with me, even to love me.

She did stop drinking. But during the final year of her life, her attitude toward me never changed. And then she was gone. The news of her death sent waves of empty echoes throughout my being as reality slammed its door in the face of hope. I would never know a mother's love.

What is wrong with me that makes me so wretched that even my own mother couldn't love me? I cried out to God.

For a brief time, I was bound up with sorrow and self. But my Father was calling to me, and it was time, once again, to make a choice. Would I be angry, or would I gladly receive what my Lord sent? I wanted to embrace His will, but how could I?

This seemed so hard. On the other hand, how could I, who had been so blessed, continue in sorrow over the one thing God had withheld from me? Was I a spoiled child crying for the only trinket on the shelf that I had been denied?

God reminded me of my promise to Him nine years before. "Though You slay me, yet will I trust You." My broken heart surrendered to him.

"O God," I prayed, "You have been my Father for ten years now. Could you be my mother too? I know from Your Word and from my experience that You are all-sufficient and that You do not withhold any good thing from Your children. Right now, Father, I give You my desire for a mother. Consume it on Your holy altar. May it be a sweet-smelling savor unto You. Continue to do unto me as it pleases You."

God accepted the offering of my desire. In a flash, it was consumed. I walked away from the ashes of that sacrifice with renewed peace and the transforming knowledge that the Father, God, is all I need.

God Moves in a Mysterious Way

God moves in a mysterious way
His wonders to perform;
He plants His footsteps in the sea
And rides upon the storm.

You fearful saints, fresh courage take:
The clouds you so much dread
Are big with mercy, and shall break
In blessings o'er your head.

His purposes will ripen fast,
Unfolding every hour.
The bud may have a bitter taste
But sweet will be the flower.

—William Cowper

Chapter 13

Beauty for Ashes

"Taste and see that the LORD is good; blessed is the
man who takes refuge in him. Fear the LORD, you his
saints, for those who fear him lack nothing. The lions
may grow weak and hungry, but those who seek
the LORD lack no good thing" (Ps. 34:8–10).

F our spirited, inquisitive little ones kept me pleas-
antly busy and preoccupied with the task of
being a mother. In all of the buzz of our lively household, I
soon forgot about my offered-up desires and surrendered
dreams for a mother. I had children to train for God and
diapers to change. There was little time for personal reflection.

But God never forgets. And in His time, He raised
out of the ashes of my childhood the most beautifully
enchanting miracle of my life. *El Shaddai,* the Strengthener
and Satisfier of His people, gave me the very thing He had
enabled me to cheerfully relinquish. He gave me a mother.

It all started with a letter . . .

It was autumn 1988, and a new radio program,
Gateway To Joy, was aired in our area. I was captivated
initially by the encouraging theme of the broadcast: Every
circumstance, if given to God, can become our "gateway to
joy." How well I knew that to be true! The opening words
of the program were a repeated source of comfort and confidence to me. "You are loved with an everlasting love—

that's what the Bible says—and underneath are the ever-lasting arms. This is your friend, Elisabeth Elliot." After just a few days of listening to the wisdom-saturated teaching of this godly woman, I felt compelled to write to her. The sensible, compassionate manner with which she taught had captured my heart.

I felt shy about writing to a broadcaster (something I had never done before) and wrestled with the idea for days before finally submitting to it. "Lord," I prayed, "help me to write an encouraging letter to this servant of Yours. She is teaching me Your Holy Word. Give me the words to thank her."

Late that night while my family slept, I wrote a brief note to Elisabeth, thanking her for giving so much of herself for the benefit of those of us who so desperately need to be taught. I was especially grateful, I told her, for her cogent teaching on abortion and the sanctity of life. I explained that the subject was especially close to my heart because my mother had wanted to abort me. I closed by telling her a little about David and the children and how God had so richly blessed our lives.

As I slipped the letter into an envelope, I decided to include a recent photograph of the children. "When I look into these precious faces," I wrote, "I realize a little of how much would have been lost had my mother aborted me."

In a few weeks I received a letter from Elisabeth. I was touched by the kindness of this busy woman, who had taken the time to write to me. Over and over again I read her words, finding strength in them and encouragement to serve God in my appointed place.

"I am so glad," Elisabeth wrote, "that you understand your job as a mother is the job that God has given you to do. What could be more glorious than serving Him, in any way at all that He appoints us to do? And surely there is no more high and holy calling than that of being a coopera-tor with God in motherhood."

She had enclosed with her letter prayer cards for each of the children signed on the back "from Elisabeth Elliot—1988." So I wrote back, including notes of thanks from the children and pictures they had colored for her.

Before long, another letter came from Elisabeth, this one with a request: "Pray that I may walk worthy of the Lord unto all meeting of His wishes."

So our family began praying daily for her—for her ministry and her personal walk with God. She prayed for us, too, and that knowledge brought strength and joy to us.

It was thus that He "who is able to do immeasurably more than all we ask or imagine" (Eph. 3:20) provided for me a spiritual mother. I was shot through with joy, thrilled in a way that only those who have grown up motherless could understand. "My gracious Father, however do You think up such marvelous things? Thank You for this exceedingly great gift to us."

Through the years I have absorbed as much as possi-ble of Elisabeth's teaching. Through her talks, her books and her personal letters, she has inspired me to give "all that I am, all that I have, all that I do and all that I suffer" to God. She has been like the dearest of mothers to me—teaching, comforting, helping, reproving, pointing me always to the cross and demonstrating to me with her life the selflessness of godliness.

Once again, God had performed an infinite act of grace, giving me beauty instead of ashes, crowning with lovingkindness and tender mercy my redeemed, overflowing life.

I sometimes reflect on my birth mother's desire to abort me. I do not blame her. Life would have been so much easier without me. But God had a plan for me. How thankful I am that she let Him have His way! I know her life and the lives of my father and sister were harder because of it. Knowing that brings me deep sorrow and remorse.

My life was difficult, too, but my Father is greater than any difficulty.

I have heard people argue for abortion "because the child would be better off never to see life than to be abused and violated. It is better to be dead than unwanted," they say. May I offer my life—and the lives of my children—as a contradiction to that argument?

"Praise the LORD, O my soul; all my inmost being, praise his holy name. Praise the LORD, O my soul, and forget not all his benefits—who forgives all your sins and heals all your diseases, who redeems your life from the pit and crowns you with love and compassion, who satisfies your desires with good things" (Ps. 103:1–5).